Dream Quest Dictionary

Gloria W. Nye

Spiral Press

Rockwood, ON Canada

Acknowledgments

Thanks to the following writers for their Haiku poetry:

Huck Leonard
Nora Leonard
Shirley Leonard
Linda Mazuranic,
Alberta Nye
Gloria Nye
Joyce Nye
Amy Palmer

Many thanks to Ruth Cunningham for permission to share excerpts from *Mystical Verses*. To read more about Ruth and her work, go to: www.self-to-self.com

A huge thank you to Jerry and Esther Hicks for bringing us the wisdom, love and joy of Abraham.

Thanks to Landmark Education for offering me the tools to live the life I love.

And heaps of thanks to my sister, Alberta, for her continual support and encouragement and for bringing me unending cups of tea to my computer.

My Dream—My Self

I look at you—veiled symbols
dancing beneath closed eyes.

I stand before you with a curious mind,
an open heart, and a questing spirit.

Teach me, enlighten me, give me your pearls.

Gloria Nye

Table of Contents

"Our nights are made for dreams,
and days for fulfilling them."

Chinese Proverb

On a chronicled journey

where time disappears

in a journey of joys,

hopes and fears.

The Listener

Ruth Cunningham

Frequently Asked Questions

What are dreams?

Dreams are messages from ourselves to ourselves. It might be difficult to believe, but we are the maker of our dreams. Dreams do not magically appear, even though at times they might seem to. And in the morning we ask ourselves, "where did *that* come from?"

Nevertheless, *we* are the scriptwriter, the producer, the director, the makeup artist, set designer, and each of the actors in our dreams—those nighttime movies that we create every night . . . and sometimes, in the daytime.

Why did we create each person, each object and each action in our dream? Dreams are the way our inner self communicates with us. In our waking lives, we are adept at hiding things from ourselves, but our subconscious or inner self knows all about us, and speaks to us through our dreams.

Why study dreams?

We can learn much from the study of dreams. Exploring the meaning of our dreams is a fascinating and rich experience, which offers new insights and awarenesses about ourselves and our lives.

What are the benefits of dream study?

Some of the benefits from delving into your dreams to find what they are telling or showing you are to:

* find answers to challenging problems
* receive inspiration and creative ideas
* identify what you really want
* heal old wounds and resentments
* work through painful relationships
* glean hints about the future
* challenge or confirm waking life decisions
* experience flying and other impossible physical acts
* rendezvous with any person, dead or alive

Why use a dream dictionary?

Dream dictionaries give common meanings that a culture shares, however, the object or person in our dreams can symbolize something else and a good dream dictionary will give you many choices to consider.

Also, our dream self like to use puns and homonyms: bear—bare; coffin—coughin', so using a dream dictionary can give you more clues and suggestions about what your dream means.

Does this Dictionary offer more than one definition?

Absolutely! Just as in any dictionary—dream or otherwise—you will find many choices as to what a particular symbol might mean.

However, since each dream contains your own personal meaning, as you read the various definitions, think or ask yourself, "Which one fits my dream?" At times, the meaning that is relevant will "jump right off the page" , or "ring a bell" reminding you of something in your waking life. You get that "ah ha" feeling, and just *know* that is it.

Can a symbol have multiple meanings?

Yes. Dreams are multi-layered and a person or object in your dream can have many different meanings. You are the judge as to which meaning fits. Sometimes a dream is so powerful that you can't get it out of your mind, and after one day of exploring one aspect of it, you can look up that same symbol on another day and get further meanings for it.

Every dream is personal. For example: four people dream about a dog. One is a veterinarian, another is contemplating getting a dog, another hates dogs, and the last person's dog just died. Dreaming about a dog would be significantly different for each of these people.

How can I find my own personal meaning?

Effective dream workers listen to their intuition. The word *in tuition* means tuition—or learning—from within. If you pay attention to your intuition—that gut feeling, hunch, or sense of knowing—you will be better able to understand what your dreams mean.

But sometimes, even the most intuitive will scratch their head and wonder what it means? And what if you think you're not intuitive? What then?

The *Dream Quest Dictionary* has a unique feature which can help you, not only understand what your dreams mean, but help you develop your intuition.

What is this unique feature?

This is the use of questions. The original dictionary grew out of the *Dream Quest Cards* which uses questions to interpret your dreams. Dream dictionaries traditionally tell you what your dream means, but *Dream Quest*—acknowledging you as the creator of your dreams—asks you what they means.

The purpose of the questions in the dictionary is to focus your attention in a suggestive and open-ended manner thus leading you to your own answers and personal associations. You can also use the question as a jump-off point and make up your own relevant questions.

What if I come up with my own meaning?

That's wonderful. Each dream is your own creation, and ultimately, you are the only one who knows what the dream means. The more you work with your dreams—especially using the *Dream Quest Dictionary* and the *Dream Quest Cards*—the more you will start making your own connections as to what your symbols mean.

For example a young woman began dreaming of an past boyfriend, and as much as she explored, she couldn't figure out what he was doing in her dreams. From keeping a dream journal, however, she could see that every time she had a dream about him, something specific was happening in her waking life, and it soon became apparent why he was making an appearance. The boyfriend had a mixture of qualities that her parents had; he was critical like her mother and gentle like her father. Once she realized that he represented her parents, it became obvious that she had used him as a symbol of her family dynamics. After that, whenever, she dreamt of him, she knew there was some family issue that needed attention.

When you discover your own meanings, it's a good idea to make a note of it in your dream journal or add it to this dictionary for easy access.

The more you use the *Dream Quest Dictionary* and the *Dream Quest Cards*, the more you develop the ability to use your intuition and listen to your inner self.

Should I keep a dream journal?

It is recommended that you keep a dream journal. The very act of writing out your dreams increases recall. Also, by jotting down what is happening in your daily life, you can more easily see the connections between your dreams and waking life.

When you write out your dreams, use present tense. "I *am* walking in the forest." This brings back the emotional content of the dream which is at the heart of the meaning.

It is also a good idea to title your dreams. This will prompt you to identify the central theme or significant part. A simple three-ring binder and lined paper works well, or you can purchase a special journal just for your dreams.

How can I remember my dreams better?

People vary in their ability to remember their dreams. When we don't remember them, we think we haven't dreamt, but we dream every night. The more you intend to remember, the more you do and reading books about dreams help.

Also, if you have a tall glass of water before bedtime, there is a good chance that nature will awaken you in the middle of the night, and in that half-asleep state, you will probably remember the dream you were just having.

Another way is to keep a paper and pen beside your bed. As soon as you awaken, scribble down anything you remember, even if it is a snippet, or a feeling. Later in the day, or that evening, you can write the dream out fully in your journal.

Don't rely on thinking you will remember the dream, especially in the middle of the night. Write something down, even one word, which can be a trigger to bring back the whole dream when you read it in the morning.

What about recurring dreams?

Recurring dreams mean you haven't got the full message yet. Your inner self will keep sending you the same or a similar dream until you get it. A journal is useful to keep track of these.

What about nightmares?

A nightmare can have many meanings. It could mean there is conflict in your life or there is something that you are afraid of confronting. Nightmares also shake us out of complacency. They get the adrenaline flowing in a physically safe manner where you can test how brave you are by facing the monster.

One woman had a scary dream about her husband surrounded by large wild cats—tigers, lions and cheetahs. She looked up *cat* in the *Dream Quest Dictionary*, reading both *pet* and *wild* and as soon as she saw "a CAT scan" it made sense. She had been worried about her husband who was going for a CAT scan the next week. She then remembered that the cats in the dream were friendly, so she relaxed.

She then wondered if the cats might also refer to her pet cat who had been acting strange for a couple of days. She took her cat to the vet who suggested a different food for it. Also her husband's CAT scan test turned out fine.

What about dreams that come true?

Dreaming of an event before it happens—a prophetic dream—is quite common. The dream mind is at a level of consciousness where time is simultaneous, so therefore, it can see ahead as well as in the past. However, future events are not written in stone. The value of keeping a dream journal is that you can check waking life events with your dreams. You may be surprised as to how many of them come true.

If you dream of a disaster, it could be precognitive, or it could be a symbol of your own fear about something. Many people dreamt of Kennedy's death before it happened. Sometimes these dreams come to prepare us emotionally for some happening. Do not be scared by such dreams, however. Be glad, that—if it is a warning—that you received it.

Let your feelings be your guide as to how you proceed and, if necessary, seek support from a family member, a friend or a professional counselor.

What about dreams of death?

If you dream of yours, or anyone else's, death, it is highly unlikely that it is referring to physical death.

A death dream usually means the death of an idea, a job, a situation, an emotional state, or a relationship—in other words, the ending of something . . . and a new beginning.

Death is a transformation from one state to another, so a dream of death could be alerting you about change. A good idea is to ask yourself what part of you or your life needs changing.

If the dream is about the physical death of someone, it could be referring to a person who is similar to—or reminds you of—the dream person.   If you know of someone in waking life who is getting ready to pass over, the dream may be a   message for you to say your goodbyes.

Can this dream dictionary be used for waking life issues?

Yes. We humans are meaning-making creatures—we make meanings out of everything.   However, an event can have different meanings for different people. A rainstorm has a different significance for the farmer than for the picnicker. The problem is we forget that we made up the meaning, so sometimes it is useful to remind ourselves what the things and events in our waking life mean.

Why do we keep attracting the same kind of person? Why did we bump into that person right at that time? Why did we choose a sports car over a sedan? Is it the influence of the media or . . . something else?

It is meaningful to discover why that object or situation is in our life and the *Dream Quest Dictionary* is a helpful tool to decipher these meanings.   Just pretend that the waking life incident or situation is a dream. (Indeed, some say it is.)

Let's say you stub your toe. Take out your *Dream Quest Dictionary* and look up *toe*. As you read the choices, you might start asking yourself some questions. Where in your life are you *towing* the line?   Are you *towing* someone or being *towed*?   And of course, consider the question for that entry: *Where are you trying to get a toe hold?*

Here's an example of how one woman used this dictionary to sort out a waking life occurrence.   After a heavy rainstorm, the woman's roof started leaking.

First, she looked up *rain*.   The question: *"Who is holding the reins?"* started her thinking. Then she looked up *roof*.   The phrase *"wanting protection"* jumped out at her. The two symbols of *rain* and *roof* seen side-by-side helped her realize that she had been letting someone control her life because she wanted protection.   Deep down, she knew this, but was afraid to admit it.   However, her waking life was showing her, just as dreams do, what was happening in her subconscious.

How does the Dream Quest Dictionary increase dream recall and my intuition?

The more you pay attention to your dreams, the better you will remember them.   Even randomly reading a few meanings from the dictionary each day will give you a good chance of remembering your dreams better.

Your intuition—tuition from within—loves questions. As soon as you ask a question, your brain/mind/body/feeling system starts looking for an answer. The more questions you ask with an expectant attitude, the more you tap into the wisdom of your inner self.

Have fun with your dreams and the DreamQuest Dictionary.

Sweeter than the honey suckle
softer than the sleeping air
bright before your dreaming eyes
our essence — tender love laid bare

September '87

Ruth Cunningham

A

maddeningly full
the moon beckons beyond
the peephole of dreams
Nora Leonard

abacus   You count for something; it is simple to calculate; there are many ways to add things up; foreign investments. *What do you need to keep track of?*

abnormal   Something out of the ordinary; you are an exceptional person. *What doesn't feel right in your life?*

aboriginal   Look at the beginning; your native country; primitive. *What is original in your life right now?*

above   As above, so below; thinks are looking up; someone lording it over you; get above the issue. *Who thinks they are better than?*

abuse   An angry person; time to say no; speak up for yourself. *In what way are you hurting yourself?*

accident   A cry to be careful; not paying attention to important matters; check your body and car for potential problems; feeling like a victim. *What did you learn from the accident?*

accounting   Something not adding up; unbalanced; there may be an error in your financial planning. *What are you not being accountable for?*

ace   Number one; the best; needing reassurance; *Who has recently been "shot down in flames"?*

ache   Someone is a pain; not paying attention to something. *What is it that you really want to do?*

acorn Abundance; spiritual growth; starting small but good potential. *Who is corny?*

acrobat   Turning yourself inside-out; trying too hard; time to relax; believe more in your abilities to perform; perhaps your expectations of yourself are a little extreme. *What or who are you falling for?*

actor   Acting a part; time to be authentic; you don't have to tell everyone everything about yourself; be truthful and honest but protect your boundaries;   describe the actors in your dream and ask yourself who they remind you of. *How are you not acting like yourself?*

add   Wanting more; put it all together; advertise what you have. *What doesn't add up?*

adultery   Something in your life has been made less or adulterated; betrayal; being cheated; a marriage that is not healthy. *Who is doing the cheating?*

adventure   A change may be indicated; consider taking the risk; explore new ideas; bored with life. *How could you make your life more adventurous?*

affair   Time to remember something; going to a fair; a fair person coming into your life. *How might you bring more excitement into a committed relationship?*

afghan   Covering things   up in a very fancy way; feeling old; needing to get cozy. *Who is hounding you?*

afraid   Life may be too dull for you; some dreams test our fears and give us ideas of how to cope; needing to handle something. *What are you afraid of?*

air conditioner   Someone needs a breath of fresh air; conditions on an inheritance. *Who needs to cool-off?*

airplane   In the clouds; flying high; you get a higher perspective of the situation; going on a trip. *Who has been feeling down?*

airport   Fast change may be indicated; someone waiting for something. *Who is leaving on a jet plane and doesn't know when they'll be back again?*

album   Old memories coming back; looking at the past; keeping track of things; Al, the   bum. *What have you stuck down and forgotten?*

alcohol   A changing state of awareness; drinking in something that changes your viewpoint; overindulgence may be indicated; caring too much about what other people think. *Who has been using alcohol to get away from it all?*

alien   Feeling strange or different; changing your self image; feeling disconnected from your people and your community; a loved one may be acting strangely, as if from another planet. *What part of yourself feels strange these days?*

allergy   Something not agreeing with you; a need to breathe deeply. *What are you doing that you don't like to do?*

alley A long narrow place in your life; don't let others bowl you over; relax and play a little; you have a friend that believes in you. *What are you approaching from the back way?*

almond   Ovaries; need healthier protein; a beautiful almond-eyed person. *Who is nuts in your life, or who are you nutty over?*

alone   Time to be still and listen; too many people around; the need to socialize; being alone doesn't mean being lonely. *Who have you cut yourself off from?*

alphabet   Out of order; too orderly; learning; start at the beginning; sending or receiving an important letter. *Where in your life do you need to get back-to-basics?*

altar   Trying to change things; worship; something sacred; making a sacrifice; wanting to be married. *What do you need to change?*

altar boy   Trying to change him; let the boy help out. *What is it that you don't like about the boy?*

aluminum foil   Vanity; distorted view; something being reflected back to you; all wrapped up; being thwarted by something flashy. *What is your dream reflecting?*

Amazon Female strength; feminism; conflict; a big book order. *Who is the warrior woman in your life?*

amber   Caution; slow down; a woman who reminds you of amber. *What or who is trapped in time?*

ambulance   Emergency; illness; health issues to look at; rushing somewhere. *What is a matter of life and death?*

ammunition   Making up stories you want to throw at people; be prepared; calling people names. *Who is being defensive?*

amputate   Not all there; a piece missing; feeling cut off. *What part do you need to get rid of?*

ancestors   Your past teaching you something; look at how you are similar to, or different from, the ancestors in your dream. *What old news has come up again for you lately?*

anchor   Time to stabilize; don't make any impulsive moves right now; something weighing you down. *What is anchoring you to your commitments?*

angel   Communication with one who has passed over; giving; kind and considerate of others; you have assistance when you need it; divine protection; being very sweet. *How are you inspired?*

anger   Covering up fear; a sense of loss; being angry instead of sad or afraid. *Who or what are you so angry at?*

angle   Try another way; nearly falling over; trickery. *What are you trying to get?*

animal   listen to your instincts or intuition more; a message about your body; describe the animal. *What part of yourself does the animal remind you of?*

ankh   A connection with Egypt; symbol of life or soul; someone who wears an ankh. *What does your soul want?*

ankle   Attach yourself to whatever grounds you; something is bothering you that won't go away; being stopped from moving forward. *How flexible is your stance?*

anniversary   Something important that happens once a year; buy yourself some flowers. *What have you forgotten?*

aunt   You are either working too much or not enough; industry; working hard; diligence; goal-oriented; feeling self important. (see **aunt**) *Who is feeling antsy to get away?*

antenna   You know what's happening; your feelers are out. *How could you get better reception of an idea?*

antique   Quality; solid; family history; old valuable things coming up for you; out-of-date. *What is valuable that you have been thinking about from your past?*

anxious   Unnecessary fears and worries; a feeling that matches with a waking life situation to get your attention. *What is it that you want so much?*

apartment   Feeling separated; put in your place; someone who lives in an apartment; a part of your life. *What have you been meaning to take a part in?*

ape   Imitating someone; be yourself; swinging around. *Who are you going ape over?*

applause   Meeting a goal; achievement; needing approval; appreciating others. *Who isn't paying any attention?*

apple   Being tempted; needing more information; you have the knowledge to do whatever you need to do; feeling seduced; needing a new computer. *Who is the apple of your eye?*

appliance   Needing a tool for something; things running smoothly; time to apply yourself. *What doesn't apply to you?*

appointment   Meeting someone; furnishing your place; pointing fingers at someone; a new position. *What are you appointing yourself to do?*

apron   Mother; nurturing; dependency; time to untie or cut the binding strings; protect yourself; spending too much time in the kitchen. *What is being covered up?*

aquarium   Feeling exposed; being confined; limited; needing to set limits; living without privacy. *Where is something fishy going on?*

archer   Poor aim, not sending your message to the right place; a person born between Nov. 21 and Dec. 21. (see **arrow**) *Where have you missed the mark or hit the bull's-eye?*

arena   Competition; playing a game and winning; feeling pressure to perform; some arena in your life needs attention; performing for someone rather than being yourself. *Who isn't being a good sport?*

argument   Using reason; getting your own way; putting your point across. *Who has to be right all the time?*

ark   High energy; piece of a whole; life-saving vessel. *Who has been throwing you a curve ball?*

arm   Give someone (or yourself) a hug; feeling the need to take up arms; power; authority; the long arm of the law; reaching out to help. *Who are you keeping at arms length?*

armour   Feeling exposed; vulnerable; a career change, hiding from something; in need of protection; looking for a knight to save you. *What part of you are you covering up?*

army   Needing to find support; get others on your side of the issue; conforming to tradition; being ordered around; getting your marching papers; leaving a job. *Who is doing all the ordering around?*

arrow   Honesty; fairness; goals indicated; a good time to change direction; someone on the straight and narrow; getting pierced. (see **archer**) *Who needs to improve their aim?*

art   Think about your problem in a different way; unconventional; unusual; needing to express yourself; you like what you like; someone named Art. *How are you stifling your creativity?*

artificial   Something not real for you; false**;** get back to the natural way. *Who or what is being fake?*

ashamed   Doing something wrong;   speaking before you think things through; taking too much responsibility for others' actions; looking at what you feel guilty about and making amends; asking for forgiveness. *How do you feel about your body?*

ashes   Ending; sadness; cleansing of old wounds; burned up; time to quit smoking. *What have you discarded lately, but are having trouble letting go of?*

assassin   Getting rid of something; wanting someone out of your life; desperate. *Who are you getting to do the dirty work?*

assault   Feeling under attack; anger from someone;   someone giving you a hard time; check your salt intake. *What problem do you need to attack in your life?*

assembly line   Repetition and boredom; a change may be indicated; look at your role in the construction of something. *What needs to be put together, or taken apart?*

assignment   Feeling unprepared; having a job to do; important orders; learning to delegate. *What haven't you done that you really want to do?*

astonished   You have great gifts; don't be surprised at how well you do; there is wonder all around you. *What do you think is 'impossible'?*

astronaut   Fast get away; ungrounded; needing to spend time in inner space; protecting yourself from something in your environment. *Who is the space cadet?*

asylum   Confinement; not fitting in; social rejection; starting another crazy project; over-protecting someone. *What are you running away from?*

athlete   Exertion; physical strain; working too hard; pay attention to your physical condition. *Who is being competitive and pushing themselves to the limit?*

atom bomb   Uncontrolled anger and aggression; threat to your well-being; unreasonable; needing to leave a violent person; something feels like the end of the world. *What would you like to blow up?*

attack   Victimization; unfairly judged; vulnerable and afraid; you just might need to attack that problem   head-on; afraid of facing something. *How are you acting too passively?*

attic   High thoughts; keeping something to yourself; it's time to tell someone about it; secrets hidden in your mind. *What memories do you need to dust off and have a look at?*

auction   Uncomfortable being judged; something sold to the highest bidder. *What do you need to get rid of?*

audience   Feeling unappreciated; someone starting to pay attention to your work or contribution; show off what you have done; listen to others; being watched; performing. *Who is sitting on the sidelines, waiting to be entertained?*

audition   Performance anxiety; concern about remembering your part; you are better at something than you think you are; trying to please someone. *Who is your competition for the leading role?*

auditorium   Start listening to your inner voice; enlarge your physical, emotional and spiritual space. *Where are you having trouble listening?*

aunt   Female member of your family; someone who is like your mother, a kind friend who will listen. (see **ant**) *Who is ruining your picnic?*

author   Being directed by others; needing to pull back and write your own life story; time to update those old life scripts; you are the author of your life.   *What needs to be recorded about your life, besides your dreams, of course?*

automatic Bored; not acting consciously; losing yourself; too easy for you. *Where in your waking life do you need to pay more attention?*

automobile   Moving automatically; acting like you think you should, instead of how you want to; get into the driver's seat. (see **car**) *How are you acting like the automobile in your dream?*

autumn   Finishing something that you have enjoyed; ready to go back to school; preparing for a time of hibernation; a time of maturity; letting go of what you don't need. *What is falling down around you?*

avalanche Overwhelmed; overworked; buried under feelings difficult to express; something roaring down on you fast; it might be time for you to get moving. *What is out of control and about to bury you?*

avenue Approach or departure; passage to fame; dress up and show yourself off. *Which other avenue could you explore?*

avocado Check if you are eating the right kinds of fat; something rich and smooth; give yourself a facial. *Who is rich and full of potential?*

award Success; winning at the game of life; gaining recognition that is long deserved; receiving a prize; persevering; an award is due. *Who is the hero or heroine?*

awkward Young; feeling unsure of what to do; embarrassed. *Where do you feel out of place?*

axe Losing a job or an important position; fear and rage; you have been grinding that axe long enough, let it go; a battle-axe; trying to hack off part of yourself. What part of your life are you ready to let go?

I saw myself beyond the glass of time
I saw a certain self I thought was mine
I tried to open time's tight windowed clasp
and reach that self
just there beyond my grasp

Conversation Through the Window
Ruth Cunningham

B

creaking, clanking, roar
monster in the furnace room
hides from quiet man
Joyce Nye

baby   A new start; beginning something new; fresh and unique ideas growing; pregnancy; acting like a baby; rebirth of the self to a new awareness or higher levels; feelings, hopes; wishes; fears. *What is just beginning in your life and needs a lot of care to thrive?*

babysitter   A lot of responsibility; testing out your limitations, or control; trusting someone to care of something very important to you. *Who are you caring for?*

bachelor   Time to settle down; wanting to be free; a single-room apartment; feeling crowded.   *Who is the lonely and swinging bachelor?*

back   Something back there; time to stand up for yourself and show your backbone; ignoring an issue hoping it will go away; getting your back up; time to back up; someone coming back into your life. *What are you turning your back on?*

backpack   Wanting to get away; a lot of past stuff packed away; remembering a time when you were free. *Who is carrying a big load on their shoulders?*

backyard   Hiding something; something buried or private; something behind you that needs attention; time to relax. *Who isn't minding their own business?*

bad   Something gone sour; naughty and not nice; judging something. *What's so bad about it?*

badge   Give yourself a reward; deserving; recognition; feeling unheard or unrecognized. *What are you not honouring in yourself?*

badminton   Back and forth, back and forth; your thoughts are flying; get some exercise; stay focused on the point of the game. *Who are you going back and forth with?*

bag   You have it covered; hiding something; carrying too much stuff; feeling overworked and needing a holiday; fear of being a bag lady. *Who has been left holding the bag?*

bagel   Take your mother out to lunch; a hole-in-one; a healthy donut. *Who are you going around with?*

baggage   Time to put down the burden you are carrying; clean out a closet; feeling resentful or like a third wheel; an invitation to unpack old feelings; wanting to settle down. *What extra baggage are you carrying around?*

bagpipes   It might be time to pipe down on an issue, or speak up; someone telling you to be quiet. *Who do you know who is Scottish?*

bait   Fishing for compliments; feeling tormented; summer sport; on the spot. *What are you wanting to attract to yourself?*

bake   Something heating up; giving it time to rise; process things gradually; some things take time; remembering mom's cooking. *Who is trying to get a rise out of you?*

balance   Feeling off centre; a need to bring balance into your life; doing too much of one thing; balance your cheque book; doing too many things at once. *What does your dream suggest you do to bring you back into balance?*

balcony   Worrying about an upcoming evaluation; promotion may be indicated; giving a presentation; something hanging over you that you need to take care of. *Who needs a higher view to get a better perspective?*

bald   Fear of losing precious thoughts; feeling unduly exposed; facing the bald truth; someone being brutally honest. *How are you not being completely honest with others?*

ball   On the ball; go dancing; you feel like crying over something; it is time to get on with it and play ball. *What task do you need to screw up your courage to do?*

ball and chain   Feeling trapped; joined to something unpleasant. *What is holding you back or down?*

ballet   Take a lighter approach; feeling muscle bound; get out and dance. *Who is keeping you on your toes?*

balloon Something swelling up; check your lungs, stomach or breasts; someone full of hot air; something about to burst or pop; a party. *What are you afraid might float away from you?*

ballroom   Needing more space to move; go out and have a good time; sexuality may be indicated. *Who needs more room to express themself freely?*

bamboo   Take some time off and go fishing; a trip or association to the orient or some tropical island, gnarled knuckles. *Who in your life has bamboo furniture?*

band   Time to blow your own horn; concentrate on your own tune even while others are playing; belonging to a tribe or group; someone on the bandwagon. *How is life like a parade?*

bandage   Covering up; a sore spot; a temporary solution. *What do you need to patch up?*

bang   Change your hairstyle; something needing your attention; a surprise. *What gives you a thrill?*

banister   Need for support; balance; a reminder of a house with a banister. *When did you last slide down a bannister?*

bank   Be careful on those sharp turns; counting your pennies; money concerns; go and sit by a river; saving for a rainy day. *What, or who, are you banking on?*

banker   Figure of power; father-figure; problems related to financial security. *How is your dream-banker dashing your hopes . . . or making all your dreams come true?*

bankrupt   Fear of losing all your money; having lots; afraid of owing people. *What has always been lacking in your life?*

banquet   There is much to choose from; take your time; look at changing banks (bank-quit); lots of different food for thought; many choices. *Who is giving all the speeches?*

baptism   A new life; cleansing; making promises; a trial or ordeal. *What important new project are you starting?*

bar   Something stopping (barring) you; legal issue; alcohol consumption; unhappy and lonely; desire to let down inhibitions; time to practice your basics as at a ballet barre. *Who is having problems related to night clubs?*

barbecue   Visiting your neighbours, or having the family in; trying to keep up with the Joneses;   it's Barb's cue; feeling saucy; eating outside the home too much. *Who is feeling skewered?*

barber   People cutting off your thoughts; a close shave; a figure of power who cuts off other people's power; cutting it too close. *Who is giving you a trimming down?*

bare   showing your inner self; feeling exposed; not having enough; covers pulled off when you were dreaming. (see **bear**)   *What is missing from your life?*

bargain   Getting what you deserve; not wanting to pay the price; a fair deal. *Who is not keeping their end of the bargain?*

barge   Moving clumsily and slowly; getting tugged around; someone pushing in. *What wouldn't you touch with a barge-pole?*

barn   That down home feeling; money (hay); a messy house; a farm holiday; someone acting like a rooster or a pig. *Who lives on a farm?*

barracks   Feeling controlled; a home away from home; no privacy; a need for companions. *What pals can you count on?*

barrel   Roll it out and have some fun; run in the rain; drinking too much beer; planting time. *Who is shaped like a barrel?*

barricade   Putting up barriers; an obstruction; feeling defensive and threatened; things piling up. *Who or what are you trying to protect?*

bartender   Being served or serving ; missing your mother; a friendship of doubtful value; a need to talk to someone; a tender friend you met at a bar; alcohol. *What needs tending?*

baseball   Par of a team; fear of striking out; not having enough confidence in yourself; filling in for someone; wanting to run home. *How are your bases loaded?*

basement   That which is deep within us; unconscious impulses; a deep look within; something base; something underneath the reason given.   (see **cellar**) *What is your dream revealing to you that was previously hidden?*

basket   A time for gathering, holding, or storing; you scored; a basket case. *What are you tired of carrying around?*

bat   Going to bat for someone; having sensitive inner radar; keeping your eyes open; pangs of conscience; unacceptable thoughts; being batty. *Who, or what, are you swinging at?*

bath   Cleansing; submerge in emotions; looking after yourself; letting your worries drain away.   *What old feelings do you need to wash away?*

bathroom   Discarding; letting go; self care; hiding; secrecy and shame. *When do you feel down in the dumps?*

battery   Charged up; time for a tune-up; getting connected; a need to rest and recharge; lots of stuff being thrown at you. *Whose energy is low?*

battle   A disagreement; a need for excitement; a battle ax; internal conflict. *Who, or what, are you battling?*

bay window   Sticking yourself out there; allowing the sunshine in; eating; San Francisco. *Who might be pregnant?*

beach   On the edge of a new discovery; ready to take the plunge; waves of emotion; afraid of being washed away; being on the border of a powerful self-discovery; happy and healthy attitude about sex. *What memories does a beach have for you?*

beads   A need to string plans together so things will hang right; being overly nervous and hot; taking a steady aim. *Who do you have a bead on?*

beans   Beans can signify good luck; in high spirits; feeling low; bloated; drinking too much coffee; check out alternatives to eating meat. *What is your dream saying about where you have been recently?*

bear   Time to come out of hibernation; give yourself a big hug; you might have to bear down more firmly to get what you want; someone overbearing; feeling exposed; putting up with something. (see **bare**) *Who is having difficulties bearing-up under the circumstances?*

beard   Courage and virility; showing your true face; shy; hiding behind; sexuality indicated. *Who do you know with a beard?*

beast   Forgetting basic instincts; rough; coarse; cruel; unthinking. *Who is being beastly?*

beat   Feeling beaten; searching for something; drive away; a lower price; unconventional; feeling a desire to strike or hit; reference to music.(see **beet**) *Who needs to take a rest?*

beaver   Thinking you have to work hard; hiding behind dams; too busy; being eager; a connection with Canada. *What is your favourite childhood TV show and why?*

bed (double)   Intimacy; sharing thoughts/feelings; comfortable; safe; pay attention to your dreams. *Whose side are you on?*

bed (single)   Strong enough to do it on your own; a desire for intimacy or a relationship; planting flowers; wanting to be on your own. *How might this symbolize your desire for more independence?*

bedroom   Needing more sleep; not enough room in your bed; wanting more intimacy in your life; feeling shy.   *Who or what is stopping you from developing a more intimate relationship with yourself?*

bee   A need to stop doing so much and just be; taste the sweetness of life; someone trying to sting you; busy as a bee. *Who is trying to get something from you with honey or by being sweet?*

beer   Time to get hopping; missing your beer buddies; relax and take some time off. *Who do you know with a beer belly?*

beet   Feeling embarrassed; hot blooded; a need to get to the root of the matter; someone in a pickle. (see **beat**) *Who is feeling beat?*

beheaded   Keep your head; set your direction and go for it; acknowledge what you know; separated   thoughts on an issue. (see **decapitated**) *What do you need to give more thought to?*

bell   Saved by the bell; a momentous occasion; stopped before the task is done; an important phone call; wanting to be the belle of the ball; being called; a warning; a church bell; wedding bells. *Who, or what part of yourself, is trying to get your attention?*

belt   Holding something together; over eating; acting unfairly; a fan belt; remembering childhood punishment; keep your pants on.   *Who is in the middle?*

bench   Sitting on the sidelines too long; not getting permission to demonstrate your skills; watching life go by; needing some standard to see how you are doing. *Who are you judging?*

berry Lips as red as berries; sexuality may be indicated; picking your nourishment. (see **bury**) *What is ripe for the picking?*

betrayal   Feeling betrayed; revealing secrets; an issue of trust; time for forgiveness. *What part of yourself are you not living up to?*

Bible   Check sacred writings for guidance; feelings of guilt and shame; time to read a good book; say bye to the bull you have been putting up with. *What message does the dream Bible give you for your waking life?*

bicycle   Time to travel more slowly; a need for exercise; a cycle coming around for the second time; childhood memories. *What is it that you can't forget?*

big   A situation seems too big, or too small; you are big enough to handle it; feeling small; someone acting big or not big enough. *Where are you feeling insignificant?*

bikini   Something skimpy; not covering up much; a need to be more discreet; sexual desires; exhibitionism. *Who is being exposed?*

bill   Feeling overloaded with bills; a person named Bill; satisfying all the requirements; time to pay up; paper money; speaking with firm lips; afraid of getting the bill. *Who owes you something?*

billiards   Time to play ball; getting behind the eight ball; go for a swim. *Who has missed their cue?*

Bingo   Big win; a jackpot; check which numbers add up for you; taking a risk. *Who are you not listening to?*

binocular   There could be two ways to see a thing; something in the distance needing a closer look; getting another's viewpoint. *Who is having trouble seeing into the distance?*

bird   Your soul soars to get height and bring you peace; a prayer answered; it might be time to leave the nest; look at the thoughts flying around you; birds are spiritual dream symbols. *What has a little bird told you lately?*

birth   Something new starting – new ideas, new friends, new job; taking a long train ride; bringing forth something; pregnancy could be indicated;. *What has taken nine months to manifest?*

bisexual   Pay more attention to same sex friends; confusing sexuality and love; an invitation to look at your beliefs about sexual partners. *Who is saying bye to their sexuality?*

bishop   Sometimes it's better to move diagonally rather than head on; wise counsel; concerns about religion. *What wise counsel has your dream bishop given you?*

bite   Bitten off more than you can chew; holding back words; swallow your words; a need to nourish yourself; someone wants a piece of you; a concern gnawing at you. *hat   are you ready to sink your teeth into?*

black   Feeling down; in the black, profiting; afraid of the dark; hidden; nighttime; containing all colours. *Who wears black?*

blackbird   Dark thoughts may be bothering you; bake or eat a pie; let the black thoughts fly away; spiritual message. *What black memories are circling?*

blackboard   School days; having trouble seeing what's written; something special to learn. *What special message is written on the dream blackboard for you?*

blade   Cutting remarks; cut something, or someone off; sharp and witty. *Who is the dashing man?*

blame   Feeling sorry for yourself; victim attitude; finding fault; a prompt to look at the other side; feeling unjustly blamed.   *Who is getting all the blame?*

blanket Something being covered up; hiding under a blanket; needing protection; someone pulled the covers off you. *Who or what do you use for your security blanket and when do you need it the most?*

bleeding   Losing something precious and life-giving; suffering; sorrow; using the whole page; not pregnant; giving more than you can afford. *Who is the bleeding heart?*

blind   Something you are not seeing; lack of understanding; hiding to catch something; a trip to Venice; not seeing the obvious. *Who is in a blind rage?*

blizzard   A storm of emotion around you; stinging words hurtled; cold; feeling buffeted. *How can you calm the confusion around you?*

block   Building piece by piece; obstruction; blocking something off; selling; compartmentalizing; standing up to someone; dense. *When did you last play with blocks?*

blood   Threatened and enraged; early sexual experience; wish or fear of pregnancy; family ties; be careful where you put your energy (life's blood). *What do you need to be shocked into accepting?*

Bloody Mary   Alcohol which is seemingly harmless; great for hangovers; rage and addiction. *Who is drinking too much?*

blossom   In full bloom; opening up; fully developed. *What is beginning to blossom in your life?*

blouse   Covering up; being modest; loose; not tidy; sailor clothes. *When or where do you wear blouses?*

blow   Leave quickly; currents of emotion; full of hot air; somebody dropping by; forget the whole thing; explode; get angry. *Who has made a mess of things?*

blue   True blue friends; peace and tranquility; bluebird of happiness; unexpected news; indecent jokes. *Who is feeling sad?*

board   Boredom; dive in; a person on a board; neglecting something; paying for your meals. *Who is not being above board?*

boat   Riding on the surface of your emotions; missing the boat; in with someone; travel. *Who isn't in any hurry?*

body   The main part; keeping it all together; body and soul; having a lewd or raucous time; appreciate your body; wanting another body; not liking something about your body; a health message. *Who is the busy body in your life?*

boil   Something hot; someone ready to bubble over; reducing something; a sore spot. *Who is boiling mad?*

bomb   Someone ready to explode; feeling bombed-out; be a comfort (a balm) to someone; fear of annihilation.   *How can you defuse the situation?*

bone   Needing to face the bare bones of an issue; bone tired; study up on something extra hard; do not hesitate; follow your intuition.   *Who do you have a bone to pick with?*

bonnet   The past can teach us; look for that bee (thought) hiding in your bonnet; sun protection.   *Who is the old-fashioned girl or woman?*

book   New knowledge coming to you; making an appointment; someone who goes by the book; in your opinion; punishment; in or out of favor with someone; a person not in your good books; keep your eye open for that special book. *What book have you read lately that is particularly significant?*

bookmark   A special book to look at; mark your spot; special day; a favourite website. *What book have you marked that you need to return to?*

boot   Computer addicted; check what's in your car trunk; dependent; someone with a high opinion of themselves; walking a long distance. *Who needs to be given the boot?*

border   On the edge of something; a dividing line; getting close. *Who has been overstepping their boundaries?*

boss   Telling someone what to do; being irresponsible, and wanting someone else to make decisions for you; father may be indicated; overworking. *How does your boss remind you of your father or mother, and how is that causing you to act inappropriately?*

bottle   Don't bottle it up any longer; sending out a call for help and hoping someone will pick it up; being stuck as in a bottleneck; concerns about a baby. *Who are you afraid is going to start drinking again?*

bottom   The foundation of something; discover the source; on your way up; underneath something; feelings of superiority; feeling down. *Who's up there?*

bounce   Watch those cheques; something coming back to you; lots of energy, or lack of energy; kicked out of something; getting the static out; too much static in your life. *What is continually going up and down in your life?*

bouquet   Time to have something sweet-smelling and special in your life; smelling something bad; a celebration. *Who deserves a bouquet today?*

bow   Buying a present for someone; shooting arrows; getting pulled taut. (see **boyfriend**) *Who is pulling your strings?*

bowl   A container: hold onto it; a night out; feminine symbol of holding, and taking care of; feeling bowled over; things all mixed up. *Where do you feel that you have been knocked off your pins?*

box   A box seat; a present; opening Pandora's Box; curiosity satisfied; a square person; cubed. *What is boxing you in?*

boy   Younger, vulnerable self; remember or imagine feeling like a boy; excited and energized about something; about a boy;   going where the boys are. (see **buoy**) *How is a situation from childhood repeating in your life?*

boyfriend   Be a good friend to your masculine side; someone back in town; an inner, balancing point of view. *Who is the new boyfriend?*

bracelet   Let someone brace you up (brace-let); punishment; a special gift. *Who, or what, is handcuffing you?*

bragging   Overly self critical; compensating for feelings of inferiority; needing the approval of others to feel okay. *Who is being overly modest?*

braid   Weave together all the strings for a tidy whole; three coming together; a braided rug. *When did you wear braids?*

brain   Computer; eager about something; getting the answers; a need to think about something: not using their brain; a smart person. *Who thinks they have all the answers?*

brake   Slow down; check your brakes; be released; watch where you are going. (see **break**) *What is about to break?*

branch   A good time to branch out or branch off; a subsidiary of the main plant. *Who is out on a limb?*

bread   The staff of life; money concerns; be sure your bread is buttered on the right side. *Who is well-bred?*

break   A time to go for it; trying something new; put an end to something; heartbreak. (see **brake**) *Who seems to be getting all the lucky breaks?*

breast   Needing some mother love; wanting comfort, worries about health; sexuality. *Who needs to confess something?*

breath   Out of breath; take time to catch your breath; speaking too quietly or afraid to speak out as in under your breath; someone needing a change of scene; get a breath of fresh air; saying contradictory things; holding your breath in anticipation; something spectacular. *How are you wasting your breath?*

breathe   Relax; breathe new life into something; keeping a secret, not breathing a word, take in energy. *Who or what is breathing down your neck?*

bribe   Needing something that you are willing to pay anything for; illegal' or unethical activity; trying to get something the easy way. *Where are you being coaxed into something you don't really want to do?*

brick   Someone in your environment who is thick as a brick; don't brick yourself in; building a solid foundation. *Who can you really count on?*

bride   A new beginning; starting over; changing from girl to woman; wanting to recreate earlier happiness as a newlywed; joining with another for a long time. *Where else do you wear white?*

bridegroom   Taking the leap; feelings about commitment; wanting to be married. *Who does the dream bridegroom remind you of?*

bridge   Time for a reunion; cross over to the other side to see their point of view; join both sides; tempted to burn your bridges; bridging the dream message to waking life. *Who is holding the winning hand?*

bright   Spiritual dream; new awareness; shining in the dark; quick-witted; all that glitters is not gold. *Who is the bright star?*

brocade   Dress up; fancy ball; all dressed up, but no place to go. *Who are you trying to impress?*

broom   time to make a clean sweep of it; get rid of old stuff; a visit to the West Coat. *Who is the wise woman in your midst?*

broken   Something finished; time you got over it; a broken heart. (see **break**) *Who has a brother named Ken (bro-Ken)?*

brooch   Being stuck; getting pinned; broach the subject with sensitivity. *What is the catch?*

brother   A close friend; brotherhood; loyalty; pointing to an issue or concern with your brother; dream brother may be representing your true feelings and situation. *Who is like a brother to you, or who is like your brother?*

brown   Browned-off (annoyed) with someone; earthy; basic; cozying up to the boss. *Who is scoring Brownie points?*

brush   Something being brushed away might need your further consideration; given the brush-off; hiding in the brush; untangle your confusion. *What do you need to brush up on?*

bubble   You have thin protection around you; something is bubbling up and getting hot. *Who is living in a bubble?*

bubble gum   Chewing away on something; memories of childhood; blowing hot air; mulling things over, but not taking anything in. *Who hangs onto things too long?*

buck   Male sexuality; being thrown off your position; time to buck up; someone passing the buck; money matters. *What are you resisting?*

bucket   Check if there is a hole in your bucket; enjoy those new bucket seats; don't try to buck it. *What are you constantly refilling?*

buckle   Check what needs to be more securely fastened; someone bent out of shape; childhood fear of punishment. *What do you need to buckle down to?*

buffalo   Puzzled; intimidated; extinct; getting stampeded; white buffalo in Native North American tradition is the dream holder. *What are you nostalgic to experience?*

bug   Letting things bug you; be sure you are not overheard; time to take care of tiny details; instinctual urges. *Who is bugging you?*

bugle   Time to wake up; a pal from the forces; a strong signal to take action. *How do you wake up?*

building   Time to build on what has happened; coming to a conclusion; look at the basic structure; preparing for something. *What are you building toward?*

bulb   Bright new ideas; a new start; something has potential to get a lot bigger; a new invention. *What bright idea are you not following through with?*

bull   Not telling the truth ; in the wrong place and doing damage (bull in a china shop); take the bull by the horns; take a stand; take time to stop and chat; stubborn. *Who is the Taurus in your life?*

bull dog   Don't let go; wrestling the problem down; a stubborn dog. *Who is getting old and stubborn?*

bullet   Hitting the mark; shooting your mouth off too soon; moving quickly. *What do you want a magic bullet for?*

bull's eye   You are spot on; you did it; feeling competitive; being on the spot; aim high. *What are you aiming for?*

bully   Good for you; shadow side of the warrior, which comes out when fear is denied; feeling victimized. *What do you have to prove?*

bum   Tired out; you've had enough; just hanging around; seeing the back or end of someone. *Who is getting the bum's rush?*

bun   severe; someone needs some sweetening; not the main course; luncheons; pregnancy may be indicated. *Who has nice buns?*

bungalow   All on one level; someone who lives in a bungalow; don't bungle it. *Who lives in a bungalow?*

bunk   Staying over; a pack of lies; two layers of meaning. *Who is bunking with you?*

buoy   Bouncing around on top of things; in the midst of a sea of emotion; lighting or sounding the way; guidance; getting knocked around. (see **boy**) *What or who is warning you not to go that way?*

bureau   storing your identity; weathering a storm; changing your image. *Who is being investigated?*

burglar   Stealing energy or time from yourself or your family; deceit; taking what's not yours. *What is being stolen from you?*

burlesque   Teasing; stripping away the surface; promiscuous; attention seeking. *What is not being taken seriously?*

burn   Mad; time to burn your bridges and move on; treated unfairly; exercising strenuously; hot tempered; sexual passion; destruction; high fever; hot under the collar. *Who is suffering from burn-out?*

bury   Time to dig up those old feelings and deal with them; denial; hiding something; forgetting the past; wishing someone dead; feeling overwhelmed and anxious. (see **berry**) *What has been revived?*

bus   going along with the crowd; a kiss; not being in control of the direction or speed of your journey; a social ride; a bus trip; someone else in the driver's seat. *Who rides a bus a lot?*

bush   Hiding out; afraid of coming straight to the point; tired out. *Who craves the uncivilized, and the wild?*

butcher   A cut up; a cruel person; pent-up anger; taking things apart. *What is being butchered?*

butterfly   transformation; unfolding; taking many forms; socially flitting around; dressed beautifully. *Who is trying to cut down on their butter?*

button   Keeping a secret; taking it on the chin; mushrooms; someone pressing your buttons. *What do you need to hold it altogether?*

"Dreams are just manifestations of what you've been thinking and feeling."

Abraham-Hicks

C

lids closed, eyes flutter
pictures, people dance about
caught in dream magic
Gloria Nye

cab   Wanting to go somewhere fast; being driven by someone else; someone else leading the way; a truck driver. *What part of your life are you allowing someone else to be in the driver's seat?*

cabbage   Inexpensive food sometimes associated with poverty; Cabbage Patch dolls; an illusion of where babies come from; Cabbage Town, trendy section of Toronto. *Who repeats themself?*

cabin   Needing to get away by yourself; time to simplify your life; a cabin cruiser. *Who drives a cab?*

cactus   A prickly person; someone who stores up emotion (water); associated with desert; barren; dry. *Whose thorns are out?*

cafeteria   Choosing what you want in life; lots of variety; let someone else do the cooking; eating on the run; yearning for a home cooked meal. *Who do you know who eats in a cafeteria?*

cage   Feeling caged; trapped; being cagey about something; locking something up. *Who or what are you protecting?*

cake   Time to celebrate; eating sweets; something is a piece of cake; wanting to have your cake and eat it too. *What is going to sell like hot cakes?*

calendar   Time will not wait, do it now; a busy social schedule; remembering a special day. *What's coming up on your calendar that you might be anxious about?*

call   A part of you calling to you; listen to the call; a call-girl; someone given a calling down; being called to make a change; someone else calling the shots; needing to call someone;   being on call; always within call; leaving your calling card. *What have you felt a calling to do?*

camcorder Keeping track of events; a desire to be a cinematographer; being more comfortable behind the scenes; keeping memories intact for posterity. *Who is hiding behind a camera?*

camel   Needing more water; watch your salt intake; cigarettes; artist's paintbrush; someone who carries the burden. *What is coming up that you are going to need a lot of endurance for?*

camera   Showing you a picture of something; look at the past for some clues; still in the picture; don't forget your camera. *Where has time "stood still" for you?*

camp   Time for a holiday; staying in one place for an extended length of time; memories of camp; roughing it. *Who is acting in an affected, effeminate style?*

campus   Higher learning; thinking of a student; wanting to go camping with your friends. *Who is camping down in your house?*

candle A romantic dinner with your significant other,   even if it's yourself; lighting a candle for someone who has passed away; doing too much; needing to put more light on the topic. *Who can't hold a candle to what?*

candy   Too many sweets; life is sweet; a sugary-sweet person; a person named Candy. *Who is sweetly tempting you?*

cane   Needing assistance; being punished; a candy cane; going for a walk; raising Cain; a cane chair. *Who uses a cane?*

cannibal   Eating yourself up over something; time to stop stewing and take action; tearing something down to be used as spare parts. *What's eating at you?*

cannon   Check out your printer; bringing out the big guns; mad at someone; fighting in an old fashioned way. *How are you being used as ammunition?*

canoe   Time to paddle it yourself; take a nature holiday; don't rock the boat; slow but tranquil traveling. *Who would you like to go with on a romantic canoe ride?*

cap   Time to put a cap on it; being a good sport; covering a bald spot; going to someone with cap in hand. (see **lid**) *What thoughts are you covering up?*

cape   Romantic wish about the past; hiding behind your clothing; a mysterious stranger. *Who is at the point of no return as in sailing around the Cape?*

captain   You are the captain of your life; father may be indicated; taking charge; steering others; in deep water; a desire to get away. *What do you need to regain control of?*

captive   Holding a part of yourself captive; wanting a captive audience; desiring to captivate someone. *What's your payoff for keeping yourself captive?*

car   Often symbolizes our self-image, as in car advertising; also how we move through life in relationships and jobs; using your life energy to get from place to place; put on the brakes, or step on the gas; notice who is in the driver's seat; parked for too long; using your energy wisely; a car also represents your body; headlights—eyes, front and rear fenders—shoulders or hips, electrics—nervous system, car fluids —body fluids, motor—brain, etc. *What does the car in your dream tell you about how you are moving through life?*

caravan   The gypsy in you calls for adventure; following behind others; look after your car and van. *Who needs a holiday?*

card   Time to relax and play; a joker; something in the cards; a card up your sleeve; putting your cards on the table; playing with a stacked deck; acting like a card (comic); reading the future. *Which card in your wallet do you identify with?*

carnations   An occasion for flowers; buy some flowers for someone; a nation of car-lovers; reminding you when you last saw carnations. *Who has buttonholed you lately?*

carpenter   Time to rebuild or repair something; Christian spiritual symbol; working with your hands; artist with wood; plan your work and work your plan. *Who is the cut up?*

carpet   Something underfoot; take disciplined action; don't leave your pet in the car; someone who treats their car as a pet; being brought on the carpet; sweeping things under the carpet. *Who is walking all over you?*

carriage   Longing for the old days; take things more slowly; check your posture. *Who is pulling you around?*

carrot   Could be a message to get your eyes checked; eat lots of vegetables; give yourself little rewards along the way; getting engaged. *Who is impressed with diamonds?*

carry   Get help with the chores; stop pushing beyond your limits; getting carried away; believing you can carry it off; someone carrying on; you need to carry through. *Who or what is becoming a burden to you?*

cartoon   Relax and read the funnies; look at the funny side of a situation; a message from a cartoon character. *What is your favourite cartoon and why?*

carve   Forming your own destiny: be careful what you take apart, you may not be able to get it back together; carving out new plans; the head of the household. *What excess needs trimming?*

cash   Look at what is valuable to you; using   charge cards excessively; too much, or not enough, cash flow; affirmation of abundance. *How are you limiting yourself?*

casserole   Simple eating; all mixed up; convenient eating; an easy meal. *Who is coming for dinner?*

castle   It's fun to build   castles in the air but don't forget the stairways; acting like King or Queen of the Castle; feeling like a princess or prince; waiting for your prince or princess. *How is your home a castle, or how could you make it a castle?*

cat (pet)   Independence; a catty person; a CAT scan; letting the cat out of the bag; acting like a cat on a hot tin roof; look at what your personal meaning is for any particular breed; taking risks; not saying what you want to. *How many lives do you think you have?*

cat (wild)   Natural instincts; always landing on your feet; a friendly back-scratch; keep your claws in; afraid of a catastrophe. *Where do you need to act quickly and forcefully?*

catalogue   Getting things in order; you will find exactly what you want; a cat-on-a-log. *What needs ordering?*

catastrophe   Dreams will exaggerate; could be a warning; suggestions on how to handle a waking life upset. *What feelings from this dream are similar to waking life?*

catch   Time to play ball; if you don't want it, throw it away; someone on the verge of catching it (getting into trouble); speaking in catch phrases; time to catch up with something; afraid of catching something; caught in a Catch-22 situation. *What do you need to catch up on?*

caterpillar   Transformation; rolling right over things because you're bigger; when a part of you dies, a new part is reborn; creeping along; changing form; beginning stages. *What is taking a long time to achieve?*

cathedral   Something huge and awesome in your life. *When was the last time you were in a cathedral?*

cave   A place of hiding and comfort; primitive and basic; going back to Mother Earth for protection; hide away and meditate; pregnancy. *What is caving in?*

ceiling   Glass ceiling; reaching new heights; limiting yourself; the top of one level is the bottom of the next. *What are you sealing off?*

celebrity   Feeling insignificant; describe the celebrity from your dream and notice who in your life fits this description; wanting recognition. *What would you like to be famous for?*

cell   Selling something; feeling closed in; someone being punished; meditating in a quiet place; a need to communicate with your cells. (see **sell**) *Who is selling out?*

cell phone   Feeling trapped and needing to communicate; time to get a new phone; selling a phone; always on call. *Who do you call on a cell phone, or who is always calling you at a bad time?*

cellar   Hiding something from yourself; issues pushed down; in cold storage. (see **basement**) *What are you selling her?*

cello   A large instrument held between the legs that makes beautiful music; sexuality indicated; part of a team that works harmoniously together. *Who is making deep and melodious sounds?*

cement   Hard and fastened; a relationship may need some fresh cement to hold it together; something that has a strong foundation. *What are you having trouble letting go of?*

cemetery   A need to go someplace quiet and relax; letting dead things rest; someone still in mourning; needing to say goodbye. *What needs to be put to rest?*

cereal   something going on and on; never seeming to end; remember to eat a good breakfast. *What do you need to complete in order to start anew?*

ceremony   An important ritual; a celebration; doing things casually; feeling too formal. *Who is making things difficult?*

certificate Wanting to get more credentials to do what you want to do; a part of yourself deserves an award; a graduation. *How do you feel unrecognized?*

chain Look for the weak link and strengthen it; don't chain yourself in, or down; a part of your work may feel like a chain gang; notice who has sent you a necklace or bracelet; afraid of a chain reaction; a chain-smoker; be careful around a chain saw. *What or who are you chained to?*

chair something not sitting right; sit and rest awhile; sitting too long; a need for exercise; the family chairs; an upcoming meeting. *How do you feel about who is in charge?*

chalk Write it up to experience; memories of school days; association with the White Cliffs of Dover; an unpleasant white drink. *How can you erase what you wrote?*

challenge A need to face up to something in waking life; someone or something is a challenge; feeling overwhelmed. *How could you look at that problem as a challenge?*

champagne A celebration; feeling bubbly; a French connection. *What special time is coming up for you?*

change Time to change something; a change of heart works wonders; spare change; the only constant is change; in the change of life; something about to change hands; always changing the subject. *What do you want to change about yourself and why?*

chapel Time to pray for something; a church ceremony; memory of a chapel. *Who needs a song and a prayer?*

chariot   Racing madly for the future; kicking up dust; an exciting adventure. *Who or what are you carrying with such haste?*

chase   One part of you is trying to get other parts of you to pay more attention;   afraid to look at something; Chase, B.C. Who is being unfaithful, or is tempted to be unchaste?

cheap   Don't believe every little bird you hear;   spending too much money, or not enough;   something dirt cheap; acting cheaply; feeling cheap; something cheapened; a cheapskate. *What costs too much?*

checkers   Taking turns;   your time will come;   plan the moves and you can win;   play a little more; a checkered past. *Whose move is it?*

cheek   Afraid to be bold; turn the other cheek; someone cheek by jowl. *Who is taking liberties or verbally sassing you?*

cheer   Cheer up; time to toast; three cheers for you; a cheerleader. *Who needs cheering up?*

cheese   One way to catch a rat; taking pictures; needing more calcium; eating too much cheese; someone always smiling; being cheesed off. *Who is acting like the big cheese?*

chef   You can be an expert at creating a nutritious and beautiful life; being creative in the kitchen.   *Who is great at putting things together in new and exciting ways?*

cheque   Receiving money; watch how you spend; having a check list; someone needing a check up; feeling checkmated; an overdue cheque. *What do you need to check out?*

cherub   An angel is with you; someone cute and cuddly in your life. *Who has cupid shot his arrow at?*

chess   Life need not be a game of war; use your intelligence and intuition to be in a winning place. *Who is the strong, protective female in your life?*

chest   Keeping warm; breathe deeply; getting something off your chest; playing close to the chest. *What's in your storage chest?*

chesterfield   A visit; an older person who smokes; a couch potato. (see **couch**) *Who is staying over at your house?*

chestnut   A colour of hair or a horse; childhood memories; busy storing something away for the next season; Christmas memories. *What are you hoarding?*

chew   Mulling over a matter; hanging on; contemplating great truths; breaking something up until you can swallow it; not letting go; chewing gum; a friend who you chew the fat with. *What do you need to chew on before you make a decision?*

chicken   Sometimes it's smart to be scared; don't let your ego push you into things; figure out just why the heck you did cross that road; being offered chicken-feed for your services. *What are you afraid of?*

chief   The main idea or plan; look at what is most important; father relationship may be indicated. *Who's the boss?*

child   Start at the beginning again; get help when you need it; innocent; remember when you were that age and how it relates to what is going on in your present life. *What was remarkable about your childhood?*

chili   Emotions too hot or too cold; have some friends in; check your furnace; an association with Chile. *What part of you is cold?*

chime You can have your say; tell people what you think; unexpected company. *What part of yourself do you need to welcome in?*

chimney   A chimney sweep is considered good luck; perhaps it is time to have your chimney cleaned; an unexpected present. *Who is all smoke and no fire?*

chimp   Someone or some part of you acting like a monkey; copying someone else's idea. *Who's the chump?*

chin   Brave; feeling self-conscious; taking a chance; proud. *Who's taking it on the chin?*

China or **china**   A country, or a plate; something may feel foreign or mysterious to you; something beautiful, delicate and precious. *What is on your plate right now?*

Chinese restaurant   Eating out; your satisfaction doesn't last; check if you are eating enough vegetables and rice; memory of eating out. *What Chinese wisdom would be helpful to you now?*

chocolate   You deserve to have some treats; something dark and delicious; take more magnesium; the love food. *Who has given you chocolates lately?*

choice   Look at recent choices you have made; consider how you make choices; wanting the best; feeling you have no choice. *What are you being asked to choose?*

choke   Stopping yourself from what you want to say; using the Heimlich manoeuvre; all choked up about something; afraid to speak. *Who are you angry at?*

chop   Feeling hurried; breaking something off; don't chop off anything before you think it through; tired of making meals. *Who keeps cutting you off?*

chopstick   Alternate way to consume things; cut some firewood; feel awkward. *What foreign thing are you trying to take in?*

chorus   Repeating the same old song; good news; all together; a core group. *What is your refrain?*

Christ   Crucifying your values or parts of yourself to please others; loving yourself and the spirit in everyone else on the planet; in need of comforting; making a sacrifice. (see **Jesus)** *What is Christ's message to you?*

Christmas   Giving and receiving; missing someone; childhood memories; seeing family; love; strong emotional reaction.   *What are you wishing for with all your heart?*

church   Worship; tired of sitting still and listening to others speak; time to pray. *When were you last in church?*

churn   Something being pounded and worked into mush; repeated motion and sound; churning out the same old stuff. *What is making your stomach churn?*

cigar   Sometimes a cigar is just a cigar; or it could be a phallic symbol; chewing on something.   *Who do you know who smokes a cigar?*

cigarette   Trying to break a habit; saying how you feel may be clearer than sending smoke signals; needing to take a deep breath; believing in ads that smoking is cool; craving something. *What else are you addicted to?*

cinema   Time to give up the act; you can be anyone you want to be; pick a role; being angry at someone for doing the very same thing you do (called projecting); larger than life. *What illusion are you caught up in?*

circle   Complete; whole; no beginning and no ending; get together with a group of supporting friends; coming full circle; repeating patterns; going in circles; a vicious circle. *What is going around and around in your life?*

circus   Life feeling like a three-ring circus; performing; flying high; nervous about your turn in the ring; traveling without roots. *Who is clowning around?*

city   Busy place with a lot happening; anonymity; industry; a city slicker. *Who needs more stimulation?*

city hall   Being judged; place of counsel; laws passed; feeling you can't win. *What have you been struggling with or fighting in vain?*

clam   Time to open up and say what you think; if you have been talking too much, maybe you should clam up for a while. *Who has clammy hands from fear?*

class   Time to hit the books; something needing to be studied; a classy person; feeling stuck with a certain group. *What test are you preparing for?*

classmate   Remembering past classmates; married to your education; you may feel stuck with a certain group of people you want to get away from. *Who does the classmate in your dream remind you of in your life now?*

claw   Grasping to get something; let go and it will come; hanging on for dear life. *Who has their claws into you?*

clay   Stand on solid ground and you won't sink; look closely at your idols; someone with feet of clay; sculptor. *Who is being used as a clay pigeon?*

clean   Time to clean up; being too concerned with germs; being clean cut and straight; make a clean break of it; time to come clean; make a clean sweep of it all. *What part of you feels dirty?*

clergy   Authority; seek advice when you need it; needing a connection. *How have your views on religion changed?*

clerk   Demanding good service; tired of waiting in line; bothered with too much paperwork; wanting to serve. *Who are you serving?*

client   Wanting more business; someone valued; feel responsible to. *What client are you treating as a friend and vice versa?*

cliff   Evaluate the risk; someone named Cliff; a fear of heights; liking cliff-hangers(apartment dwellers); taking a chance. *Who likes to live on the edge?*

climb   Moving up; climbing down is difficult; moving toward something or away from something; success if going up; some setbacks if going down. *What are you climbing for?*

cloak   Attempting to cover up; sneak in for the attack; a cloak-and-dagger approach; hiding yourself. *Who is pining for the past?*

clock   Time passing too quickly ; act now; make your own time; a clock-watcher; doing something round the clock; going like clockwork; clocking in. *(*see **time***) What are you spending too much time on?*

close   Completion; moving on with things; living in close quarters; someone close-fisted; close-mouthed about something; a close shave; closing your eyes to something; feeling as if things are closing in. (see **clothes**) *Who or what do you need to shut the door on?*

closet   Wanting to hide; hiding something; time to clear out your closets' a private person. *What are you afraid to tell?*

cloth   Material concerns; you can make a new garment (a new self) with new cloth; someone   just like you; rough or smooth cloth; a person of cloth (religious figure). *Who is cut from the same cloth?*

clothes   Your identity; changing self-image; a clothes-horse; wearing comfortable clothes; changing your style. (see **close**) *What do clothes mean to you?*

cloud   Come down out of the clouds and put your feet on the ground; looking for the silver-lining; feeling on cloud nine; plans that are in the clouds; feeling under a cloud; one's head in the clouds; air travel. *What has clouded your vision?*

clover   A good omen; you are in the clover, or prosperity; eating greens. *Who's standing around chewing their cud wasting time?*

clown   A clown in your life; clowning around too much; wearing a mask and not being honest about sad or angry feelings. *Who is hiding behind the clown face?*

club   Joining with others can be useful; wanting to club someone; someone who eats club sandwiches; a clubhouse. *What club would you like to join?*

coach   Getting help; you can also help others in a non-judgmental way; a pal and a guide; a coach house. *How could coaching help you achieve your goals?*

coal   Dark thoughts; heat; black; dense; formed deep within; carrying coals to Newcastle (bringing something not needed); being hauled over the coals. *What is fuel for your passion?*

coast   The coast is clear; you are coasting along; a person living on the coast. *Which coast is beckoning to you?*

coat   Something needs a coating; dress warmly; hanging on by your coat-tails. *What are you covering up?*

cobweb   Home of the spider;   it is sticky and traps innocent bystanders; time to clean out the cobwebs in   your mind and get a clear, fresh perspective. *Who haven't you seen for a while?*

cockpit   A male in the pits; time to pilot yourself; take control; fear of flying. *Which male is at the controls?*

cocoa   Memories of childhood; family; dark, delicious, rich, brown, warm and yummy. *Who or what does this describe in your life?*

coconut   Watch what might be ready to fall on your head; a big nut in your life; a tropical holiday. *Who supplies warm and nutritious nutrients to you?*

cocoon   Make inner changes before venturing out; don't stay inside forever; there is a time to stretch your wings; break out and fly. *Who is all wrapped up in themselves?*

codfish   Staples; the main food of maritimers; feeding yourself well; connection with Atlantic Ocean and eastern seaboard of Canada and the United States could be indicated; cod-liver oil. *Who needs to have more patience?*

coffee   Being too stimulated by something; time to sit down and chat with a friend; talking it out over coffee; trying to cut down. *Who drinks too much coffee?*

coffin   Giving up smoking (coughing); remembering someone who has passed. (see **cough**) *What do you need to bury?*

coin   Prosperity; money;   receiving it or giving it; financial issues troubling you, good fortune coming; to coin a phrase. *Who pays a lot of attention to money, or not enough?*

cold   A part of you needs warming up; keeping things fresh; time to chill-out and enjoy; making cold-calls; getting cold feet; feeling indifferent toward someone or something; left out in the cold; acting in cold blood (without emotion); discouraged; going cold turkey; a cold-hearted person. *Who's been giving you the cold shoulder?*

college   Higher learning; something to be studied; wanting to be part of the *in* crowd. *What life dream have you left behind in college?*

colour   Put more colour and adventure into your life; your thoughts may be coloured (influenced) by another; showing your true colours; with flying colours. *Where else have you seen this colour and how do you feel when you look at it?*

column   Regimented; straight up and down; accounting concerns. *Who needs to have their backbone checked out?*

comb   Time to straighten out your thoughts on some matter; keep sifting through the details; acting as cocky as a rooster. *What are you looking for?*

combat Confrontation; struggling with things; armed forces; warring with someone. *What part of yourself are you battling?*

comedian Finding the humour in it: laugh yourself to health; nearly anything can be funny; laughing on the outside, crying on the in. *Who is being the comedian to cover up insecurities?*

comic Making it funny; remembering your childhood; look at the book you're reading for its funny side; time for some comic relief. *Who collects comic books?*

companion A friend; doing something with another person; loneliness. *Who are you going along with?*

compass Check your directions before you head out; needing direction; a magnetic pull. *What direction are you going in?*

competition Fear of failure, a challenge to overcome; make it a win-win situation; feeling insecure. *Who are you competing with?*

complaining Finding fault; feeling powerless to change things; make a list; look at ways you can improve what is bugging you. *Who are you not forgiving?*

compliment Say something nice to someone; reassurance that you are on the right track; be kind to yourself. *What compliment makes you feel good about yourself?*

composer Time to get it together; a need for some quiet time. *What is falling apart?*

computer Stored memories; listen to your emotions as well as logic; what you put in comes out; something doesn't compute; spending too much time at the computer. *What are you storing away or saving?*

conceal   Hiding something; afraid to reveal yourself; needing more sleep. *What will happen if you are found out?*

conceited   Low self-esteem; a need to feel important; showing off. *How does the dream character compare to someone in your life?*

condescending   Going down; looking down on someone; a prisoner going even further down. *What part of yourself do you not accept?*

cone   Give yourself a reward of ice cream; acting like a dunce or a witch; a triangle; childhood memories. *What do you deserve a treat for?*

conference   Call a board meeting of all your inner personalities and body parts and have a dialogue; time to talk to someone; get away for awhile; presentation; performance anxiety. *Who do you need to consult with?*

confession   Hiding something that needs to be said; freedom comes when you tell the truth; forgive yourself, forgive others. *What do you need to get off your chest?*

conflict   Parts of yourself not integrated; things are not what they appear to be; undecided. *What are you pushing away?*

conformity   Thinking for yourself, fitting in; look at where you are following the crowd; feeling stifled. *What part of you are you not allowing to grow?*

confront   A need to face up to something; fear may be indicated; a challenge; someone conning you up front. *What needs your attention right now?*

confused   A step toward new learning; not understanding something important. *How is confusion paying off for you?*

conspiracy   Look at any illegal doings around you; plotting; secrets are never really secret. *What devious plans are you up to?*

contact   Take care of the details; focus in on something (lens); give Len a call; time to see or call someone; a contact sport. *What do you need in order to see an issue more clearly?*

container   Holding onto something; time to fill up; feeling too full. *What are you containing that you could let go of?*

contest   Feeling better than or less than; pressured to do better; challenged at work; easily a winner. *Who are you in dispute with?*

contortion   Twisting yourself out of shape over someone or something; relax and straighten out. *What is all mixed up?*

control   Needing to let go; feeling unsafe and insecure; whatever you are doing tell yourself you chose it; feeling out of control; everything under control; holding a controlling interest. *What, or who, are you trying to control?*

convent   Hiding out; protection; seclusion; counsel with women. *What women in your life can give you spiritual guidance?*

conversation   Talk it over; talking too much; needing to listen; a conversation piece. *What has to be said?*

convertible   Take the top off; talk off the top of your head; change things around; get a breath of fresh air. *What needs to be converted?*

cookie   Life is sweet; give yourself some treats; watch your sugar intake; that's the way the cookie crumbles. *What girl is guiding you?*

cooking   Things getting hot; making plans; getting closer to your goals; someone cooking the books; a person's goose is cooked; cooking things up. *What's cooking?*

cop   Feeling guilty; afraid you will cop out; making a deal, as in copping a plea; authority figure symbolizing father. (see **police**) *Who is watching and judging you?*

corn   A stiff-necked person; trite; sentimental; old-fashioned; needing a place to hide; farming may be indicated; something corny. *Who is stepping on your toes?*

corner   Boxed into a corner; feeling there is no where to turn; you never know what is around the next corner. *How do you feel backed into a corner?*

coronation   A great ceremony; time to get your crown. . . . or get crowned;   an English friend; connection to Coronation Street. *Who is acting high and mighty?*

corridor   Remembering birth trauma; a rebirth; going through; a passage; staying on the straight and narrow; indicating movement. *When were you last in a corridor?*

cosmetic   Showing your inner beauty; someone may be trying to save face in a situation. *What are you covering up?*

costume   A cover-up; pretending to be someone else; dressing up; going to a party; costume jewellery. *What are your favorite clothes and where do you wear them?*

cotton Hard work; cotton candy; time to sew; cotton balls; wearing cotton clothes; natural; comfortable; breathable. *What part of your life does this describe?*

couch Lazing around; watching too much TV; picking your words carefully.(see **chesterfield**) *Who sleeps on the couch?*

cougar Wild; natural; fierce; having claws out; mountain predator. *Who is the wild cat?*

cough Afraid to say something or express yourself; forgive and bury the past (coffin); get some rest and relaxation; needing to cough up more than you can give; smoking too much. *What do you need to say to someone?*

counter Money concerns; wanting attention; serving others; opposite. *What is on your kitchen counter?*

counterfeit Not authentic; getting something for nothing; the wrong Bill; working at a counter that does not fit who you are; imitation of the real thing. *Who's the phoney?*

counting Depending on someone; repetitious; counting your chickens; counting the days; counting your blessings; not counting; losing count; out for the count. *Who keeping track?*

country Remembering your origins; a need to belong; opposite to city; getting back to nature; in unknown territory; someone from another country or wanting to live in another country. *What do you think of your own country?*

couple Two important things; joining together; two singles don't necessarily make a couple; feeling like a third wheel. *What does being a couple mean to you?*

coupon   A gift; a treat; extra money coming in; saving something. *If you were given a free coupon, what would you want it for?*

court   Pay attention to what you are doing; justice will be served; needing your day in court; lawsuit; going out on dates. *Who is acting like a royal pain?*

cover   Hiding; protecting yourself; being exposed; covering your tracks; a cover-up; time to take cover; look it over from cover to cover. *What are you covering up?*

cow   Check if you are getting sufficient calcium; country living; motherly love; not very smart; eating too much; waiting till the cows come home. *What can't you stomach?*

coward   Being a bully; afraid you won't be able to do it; being hard on yourself. *What are you afraid of?*

crab   Taking a sideways action; stop complaining; the sign of Cancer in Astrology; instinctive nurturing; protective; affectionate and romantic. *Who is crabby?*

crack   Something about to break apart; watch the wise cracks; addictions may be indicated; time to crack down on something; take a crack at it. *What has fallen between the cracks?*

cracker   Loud; going nuts; liking something a lot; Cracker Jack. *Who wouldn't you mind eating crackers in bed with?*

cradle   Warm and cozy; protected; rocked; loved; a cradle snatcher; from cradle to grave; a new beginning; hold someone or something tenderly. (see **crib**) *What do you hold dear?*

cramp   Someone cramping your style; someone in a tight spot. *What muscles are you overworking?*

crane   Look all around you;   standing tall. *What heavy thing, or thoughts, are you lifting or swinging around?*

crash Be careful; going somewhere you are not invited; look at what is about to fall on you; making a crash-landing. *Who is making the loud noises or a big fuss?*

crawl   Things are moving too slowly for you; we have to crawl before we walk and run; take each step as it comes; don't go crawling back. *Who gives you the creepy crawlies?*

crayon   Drawing on childhood memories; colourful fun times; keep it simple; draw a picture of your dream with crayons. *What is your earliest memory of crayons?*

crazy   Too much going on; over-eager and enthusiastic; think it out carefully before you act. *Who is overly stressed and worried?*

creek   Get more exercise; keep those joints oiled; a trickle of emotions; a crick in the neck; under a lot of strain; a visit to the country. *Whose bones are creaking?*

creep   Moving too slowly for you; an undesirable person in your life; you have to creep before you walk and run; creeping up on someone; something creeping up on you. *Where do you need to slow down?*

crib   Protected place; restricted eating; copying another person's work: (see **cradle**) *Who is cheating?*

crime   What we put out, we get back; something is a rotten shame. *Which law are you tempted to break?*

crocodile   Someone crying crocodile tears; a crocodile clip; in a while, crocodile; crawling on your belly; a visit to Florida. *Who keeps snapping your head off?*

crook   Stealing important things from yourself; something bent or curved; needing support in managing a bunch of sheep. *What are you hooked on?*

crooked   Dishonest; not a straight path; bent over. *Who isn't being straight?*

cross   A symbol of Christianity; bravery; illiteracy; a burden; a duty; mixing things up; a countering blow; suffering; annoyed with someone; telling a lie; hoping for the best; pledging; meeting up with someone; a new thought; taking care of details; mixed communication; a misunderstanding. *Who are you cross at?*

crow   Really happy about something; keeping straight on your path; dark thoughts flying around; a disappointing and sad message; fear of looking old.   (see **raven**)   *Where have you been made to do something disagreeable and humiliating?*

crowd   Feeling crowded; going someplace where there is a crowd; three people don't always make a crowd. *Who are you crowding?*

crown   Off the top of your head; special hat wear; rewards; head of the house; the winner; English money; feeling as if you want to crown someone. *Who is acting like royalty?*

cruel   A cruel master; being too sweet and nice all the time; doing fancy stitching (crewel). *Where are you being cruel to yourself?*

cruise   Time to take a holiday; moving along smoothly and steadily, no bumps in the road now; going at cruising speed. *Know any Tom's?*

crumb   Being left with the crumbs; you deserve more than the tiny bits left over; a finished meal. *What's crummy in your life?*

crust   Concerns about aging; hard outer coating; tough minded and insensitive; part of the upper crust. *Who is getting crusty?*

crutch   Someone using half their abilities; needing help; using something to help you move forward. *Who, or what, are you leaning on?*

cry   Feelings of despair; sadness; missing someone; feeling regret; not allowing yourself to cry; accused of being a cry-baby; crying over spilt milk; someone who cries wolf; a far cry from what you want. *Who needs a strong shoulder to cry on?*

crystal   Energy will flow if you let it; something is clear but multi-faceted; you can see through this issue but you aren't looking in the right direction; hoping for a crystal ball prophecy; receiving radio messages; someone who collects crystal. *What is becoming crystal clear to you?*

cube   Feeling boxed in; claustrophobia; someone is a real square; playing with dice; eating too much sugar. *How can you get out of the box in your thinking?*

cuckoo clock   A reminder that time is going by; get on with it. *Who is acting silly?*

cup   Something needing to be contained; someone in their cups; symbol of the feminine (chalice); something is just your cup of tea. (see **grail**) *How does your cup runneth over?*

cupboard   Closing something away; hiding something; bored with cups; storing thing. *What in your life is bare?*

cure   Healing an illness; finding a remedy for whatever ails you; aging nicely; wanting a cure-all. *Who needs to be cured?*

curl   Sliding toward a target;   time to curl up with a good book; someone is being really good, or else horrid; enough to make your hair curl. *Whose lip is curling with disgust?*

curry   Spicy issue; hot climate indicated such as India or Jamaica. *Who are you trying to curry favour with?*

curse   Repressed anger may be indicated; afraid someone has put a curse on you; a stretch of bad experiences. *Who are you cursing?*

curve   Sensuality and sexuality; what goes up must come down; feminine attraction; someone throws you a curve ball. *Where might you have to curve around something in order to reach your goal?*

cushion   wanting a soft place to rest; needing support from someone; being caught when you fall; a cushy job. W*hat could you do to cushion the blow?*

cut   Removing the parts you don't like; self-punishment; sharp and mean remarks; a cut above; not so cut-and-dried as you thought; cutbacks might affect you; cutting someone down to size; cutting it fine; time to cut the knot; feeling cut off from someone close; cutting people short; having your work cut out for you. *Who is trying to cut corners?*

cutlery   Eating properly; needing the right tools for the job; holding something steady while you examine it. *Who's worried about table manners?*

cyclone   Things spiraling toward the center; disorganized; living in a mess. *What is beginning to blow wildly out of control?*

cylinder   Male sexual symbol; container for cigars; pistons in a car engine; a rolling pin; hair curlers; a weapon; a wand; going round and round; storing things in jars. *Where do you normally see a cylinder?*

cymbal   Paying attention to symbols; waiting your turn; ring out loud and clear; be heard.. *What are you doing to get attention?*

"We are such stuff as dreams are made of,
and our little life is rounded with a sleep."

William Shakespeare

D

Wind snatching at blind
noises reaching into my dream
calling me to life
Linda Mazuranic

dad   Time to phone dad; a message from your dad; someone reminds you of him, but you hadn't noticed before. *How are you similar to your dad, or your boss?*

daffodil   Spring; Easter; a type of Narcissus. *Who is so caught up in themselves that they can't see anyone else?*

dagger   Something being pointed out to you; looking daggers at someone; needing to make your point. *Who is feeling threatened?*

dairy   Check out sources of calcium; comfort food; relationship with mother may be indicated. *Who can you go to for comfort?*

daisy   Innocent; playful; simple; country life; thinking of someone who is pushing up daisies; a name. *When did you last make a daisy chain?*

dam   Holding something back; fearing a flood of emotions; annoyed at something or someone; protecting; doing your damndest. *What is not worth a damn to you?*

dance   Keeping step; in rhythm with yourself; waiting on someone; sexuality may be indicated; moving; lively; cooperation; taking turns leading and following; to dance attendance on; dance to your own tune. *Who is dancing as fast as they can?*

dandelion   A really super lion; some think a nuisance; powerful ; something that grows plentifully. *What are you overlooking?*

danger   Take caution; needing more excitement in your life; making things scarier than they need be. *How are you in danger?*

dare   Courageous; adventuresome; fear of consequences; challenges. *Who is the daring person?*

dark   Confusion; cannot see the light of truth; night; black and dense; not seeing the dark; a dark person; someone living in the Dark Ages. *Where can you bring more light into your life?*

dart   Move away quickly; making a point; playing games. *Who is stinging you with sharp remarks?*

date   Sweet and foreign; a special time for you; out-of-date; up-to-date. *What happened in the past on this same date?*

daughter   Offspring; caring; female line; the younger feminine part of yourself. *How is your daughter like you?*

dawn   Don or Dawn; a time of special energy; new beginnings; getting an early start. *What have you just realized?*

dead   Time to let a part of you go; a dead-beat; a dead-end job; right on dead centre; someone dead from the neck up; finishing in a dead heat; traveling by dead reckoning; dead set on doing something; getting rid of the dead weight; wouldn't be seen dead with; check your dead-bolt; in a deadlock situation; a deadpan face. (see **death**) *Who is dead to the world?*

dead relatives   Loved ones who have passed over are always with you; a special message from them. *Who are you still mourning?*

deaf   Refusing to hear; turning away; words falling on deaf ears; turning a deaf ear. *What are you afraid to hear?*

death   Time to let go of old ideas or an old situation; a re-birth; sticking it out to the bitter end; feeling as sure as death about something; doing it to death.(see **dead**) *What are you afraid of?*

debt   Hung up about an old debt; time to take account of things; let it go; feeling gratitude. *Who owes you what and why?*

decapitated   Separating thoughts from feelings; cutting off good thoughts. (see **beheaded**) *Who are you losing your head over?*

decision   No decision is still a decision; listen to your feelings as well as logic; envision all the alternatives and pick the one you want. *What are you being asked to decide?*

deck   Feeling like hitting someone; a stacked deck; time to clear the decks; getting rid of clutter; summer socializing; get ready for action. *Who is holding the winning hand?*

decorate   You deserve a reward; change your house (self) in some way; add to the beauty. *Who or what do you want to decorate?*

decoy   Artificial; tempting danger; faking it. *How are you being lured?*

deep   You may have to dive deep to find the answer; some problems are deep-seated but can be resolved; going off the deep end; in deep water. *Who is being intense?*

deer   Swift; graceful; innocent; a loved one. *Who is dear to you?*

defeat   Ready to give up; reference to feet, ashamed or bothered about losing; feeling discouraged or ready to give up. *What did you gain from a defeat?*

defecate   Be generous; letting go; rid yourself of old wasteful thoughts; needing more privacy; cleaning out. *Who is uptight?*

defend   Having your guard up; protecting something; looking at the truth, no matter how painful. *What are you afraid to look at?*

defiant   Standing up for what is right; taking a challenge; refusing to obey. *Who is protesting too much?*

deformity   Something not forming the way you want it to; a part of yourself that you are rejecting. *What isn't working properly?*

defrost   Feeling less afraid of your emotions; someone has pulled the plug; (see **frozen**) *What needs to be thawed?*

delay   Procrastinating; waiting; something you want to do is held up; operating on delayed action. *What do you keep putting off?*

delinquent   Failure to do what is required; feeling guilty. *What is due but not paid?*

demon   Lots of energy and strength; in Greek mythology, an inferior or minor god; a demon for work. (see **devil**) *What demons have you created to scare yourself with?*

den   Help from the Boy Scouts; time to relax and read. *What wild person is living or working close to you?*

denim   Just a blue jeans type of gal or guy; plain; working clothes; long wearing. *Who wears denim?*

dent Starting a large job; feeling caved in. *What part of you feels dented or squashed?*

dentist Teething; beginning; chewing on something; time for a dental checkup; be clear in stating what you mean. *What empty space in you needs filling?*

depart Something or someone leaving; let it go; to take apart; start on a new course. *What do you need to let go of?*

department store Searching; organize your stuff; shopping for something or someone. *What are you storing up?*

deposit Something to be put in place; putting it down. *What needs to be put somewhere for safekeeping?*

depot Storing something valuable; meeting someone or saying goodbye. *Who do you need to recruit for help?*

depression Sinking; a storm might be on the way; sad. *What are you angry about?*

derby Going bowling; thinking stiff and unbending thoughts; a contest; an Englishman; a gambler; wishing for past excitement. *What race are you running?*

descend A downward motion; something coming on you suddenly; looking at an earlier time for the answer; lowering yourself. *What have you inherited from your parents?*

desert A dry and barren stretch in your life; wilderness; being left alone; abandoning something; Arizona. *Where are you not being intellectually stimulated?*

design   A plan; an outline of what you want to do; take action on purpose; set apart; draw the designs from your dream; having designs on someone. *How are you fashioning a life for yourself?*

desire   Feeling upset by what you are longing or craving to do; your dreams show your hidden desires. *What do you really want?*

desk   Get away from work for a while; clean up your desk; feeling desk-bound. *Who is overworked?*

dessert   Time for something sweet; good stuff follows; feeling deserted. *Who is getting their just desserts?*

destitute   Something important lacking; pay attention to the basics. *Who needs taking care of?*

destroy   Something breaking apart; the end to a situation. *What are you tempted to take apart or build up?*

detached   Coming apart; separate; uninvolved. *What do you need to release?*

detergent   Time to clean up; in the suds. *Who watches too many soaps?*

devil   An angel in disguise; look for the lesson; stuck between the devil and the deep blue sea; a devil-may-care attitude; playing devil's advocate. *(see **demon**) Who is raising hell?*

dial   Old-fashioned way to phone; getting a dial tone; trouble getting connected; needing to communicate; getting on the right wavelength; a slow way to communicate. *Who do you need to telephone?*

diamond   Hard; under a lot of pressure; time to play ball, or cards; make a commitment; play some of Neil's songs; a diamond wedding. *What is very precious to you?*

diaper   Time to clean up; cover up; protect; suggests immaturity; lack of control. *Who is acting like a baby?*

diary   Secret thoughts; keeping track; expressing yourself. *When are you going to start writing the story of your life?*

dice   A gamble; play more games; no dice. *What is chancy in your life?*

dictator   Someone telling you what to do; wanting absolute power; writing somebody else's words; feeling under the control of another. *Where do you not feel free?*

dictionary   Needing to know the meaning; put things in order; using the right word. *What do you really mean to say?*

diet   Feeling fed up; watch what you are eating; planning to dye something. *How do you feel about your body weight?*

dig   Looking deep for the answers; time to dig in and work; get with it; digging your heels in. *What have you dug up?*

dining   Nurturing yourself; the main course; eating out. *Who's eating on the run?*

dinner   Family meal; evening; formal; nurturing. *Who is coming to dinner?*

dinosaur   Spending too much time in the past; time for some new ideas. *What big thing is outdated in your life and is threatening to consume you?*

diploma   An earned reward; paper that acknowledges your work; goal achieved. *What do you want the right to do?*

dipper   Your head in the stars; dip in and take a chance. *What are you dipping into these days?*

direction   Look where you are going; following trends single-mindedly; feeling directionless. *Who is giving you directions?*

director   Giving orders; guiding others. *What would be the title of your real-life movie?*

dirt   The need to clean something up; feeling unclean; a dark side of yourself that you are keeping hidden; finding something dirt cheap; doing a person dirt; being treated like dirt; getting the dirty end of the stick; a dirty trick. *What are you feeling ashamed of?*

disability   Feeling disadvantaged; you can live a whole life; you have many abilities. *What is stopping you from doing what you want?*

disappear   Something gone from your life; a slow fading. *What are you trying to get away from?*

disapproval   Looking down on someone or some part of yourself; rejection. *What part of yourself do you want to change?*

disaster   Don't let your fears consume you; disaster dreams exaggerate to get your attention, so pay attention. *How could you have prevented the dream or waking- life disaster?*

discover   New places or avenues to explore; an upcoming opportunity;   find the real meaning in the situation. *What have you recently discovered about yourself?*

disease   Not at ease with something; an unhealthy state; resistance. *What can you do to lessen the stress?*

disgrace   Disgrace to one family is a joke in another; see the funny side. *Who is 'dis Grace anyway?*

disguise   Being something you are not; covering up; not being your authentic self. *Who do you want to be?*

dish   Taking it all in; look at what is being served to you; treating women with respect. *Who is dishing it out but can't take it?*

dishonest   Covering up; unfair; hiding something. *When or where haven't you been telling yourself the truth?*

disk   Needing to back up important information;   have your back checked out; storing something. *What could be made more compact?*

dismissal   Leaving something; time to go; you can choose what you keep. *What is your interest in missals?*

disobedient   Doing it your way; time to put some discipline in your life. *Who is over obedient or doesn't listen?*

dissect   Feeling cut in half; cutting into parts; study carefully. *What is being divided up?*

dissolve   Things are starting to flow; something starting to fade. *What is being broken up or is ending?*

distance   Going the whole way; needing some distance from someone. *What do you want that is now at a distance?*

distrust   Too trusting; doubting someone or something; trusting your gut feelings. *Who is naive?*

disturbance   Confusion; not knowing where you belong; interruptions. *What specifically is so disturbing about this dream?*

ditch   A last attempt; letting go of something; abandoned; getting dumped. *Who have you left in the lurch?*

dive   Moving headfirst; not afraid of plunging into your emotions; frequenting undesirable places. *What are you about to dive into?*

divine   Spiritual dream; divine plan for your life. *What are you inspired to do?*

divorce   You may need to break away from a union that is not working; this could be a clue that help is needed in the relationship. *What do you need to get away from for awhile?*

dizzy   Going around in circles; not seeing straight; confused; a jazz fan. *What foolish thing are you up to now?*

dock   Accused person; some part taken away; something jutting out; your ship has come in; doc. *Who is loading stuff off on you?*

doctor   Healing; tampering with; higher studies; needing to see a doctor. *What's being doctored?*

dog   God backwards; your best friend; loyalty; friendship; responsibility; learning new ways; a dog-eat-dog situation; someone/something going to the dogs; your day will come; dressing up; in the doghouse; look at breed for your personal meaning and/or the puns for each, i.e. Shepherd, retriever, dachshund (dashing around). *Who is showing off?*

doll   Plaything; practicing for the real thing; treating a woman as brainless; not alive. *Who is the doll in your life?*

dollar   Money issues; time to start saving; a day's work; frequenting dollar stores. *What did you recently buy?*

dolphin   Play and sex can be good for you; intelligence and love have many faces; come out of your element for a breath of fresh air; protection needed. *Where in your life do experience unconditional love?*

dome Thinking high and mighty thoughts; alternative housing; a roof over your head. *Where do you go that has a rounded ceiling?*

domineering   Be assertive; arrogant or overbearing person in your life; overpowering others. *Who is bossing you around?*

domino   Seeing things in black and white; take time to play. *What is about to set everything off?*

door   A new entrance, or a way out; time to show someone the door; doors open and close, they welcome and shut out; closing the door on something; going door-to-door; don't close all your doors on something; feeling like a doormat; the Doors (drug culture band). *Which way is the door swinging for you?*

doorbell   Opportunity can ring as well as knock; announcing that you are here; expecting someone. *Who do you want to visit?*

doorknob   Get a handle on it; opening something. *How can you get a better grasp on what is bothering you?*

doorway   A threshold to a new beginning; something hidden now revealed. *How are you feeling shut out?*

dope   Getting the lowdown on something; you think someone is stupid. *Who is taking something to alter their perception?*

dormitory   Many people sleeping in the same room; school days or camp days; cooperative living. *Who wants more privacy?*

double   Double-trouble; two of something; do it quickly, someone who looks like someone else; go around; go back the way you came; vision may need checking; acting twice as fast; needing to do a double-blind test; being double crossed; a double-edged deal; a double-jointed person; doubled-parked; a double-standard; doubled-up with laughter; a double-whammy. *Whose place are you taking?*

double-decker bus   Going somewhere with another person; working in partnership; England may be indicated; tourism. *Who do you like to travel with?*

dough   Needing more money; eating too many sweets; needing too much. *Who are you trying to get a rise out of?*

doughnut   take a break; nuts to money; a hole in one. *Who do you eat doughnuts with?*

dove   Peace; the Holy Ghost; a gentle, innocent, loving person; a pigeon in disguise. *Who is doing all the squabbling or cooing?*

down   Delving deep; getting rid of something; feeling low; down and out; a down payment; a down-to-earth approach; three chances to get ten yards; soft and cozy; afraid of the downfall; going downhill. *What has been handed down to you?*

drag   Something getting you down; dragging one's feet; dragging something out to make it last longer; a drag queen; feeling as if you have been dragged through the mud; someone being a drag on you. *What past emotional pain has been dragged up lately?*

dragon   Considered good luck for the East, bad luck for the West; a strong chaperon, someone lagging behind. *Who is breathing smoke and fire?*

drain   Time to let it go; drained of energy; drained to the last drop; something gone down the drain. *What has become a drain on you?*

drama   Pretending things are different; getting caught up with your own scenario; an old script. *Who is being overly dramatic?*

drape   Covering things up; hiding behind. *What are you arranging so carefully?*

draw   Pulling up, or out;   attracting something   to you; making pictures; making demands; being a drain; breathing in; taking money; neither side wins; approach one; arrange in order; draw a bead on someone;   drawing someone's fire;   setting your limits; drawing something out for too long; drawing on friends for help; being quick on the draw. *Who do you need to draw the line on?*

dream   There are many layers to dreaming; sometimes we have a dream within a dream; dreaming up new plans.   *What are you having trouble waking up to?*

dress   Time to change your identity or remove some part of it; time to dress up and have fun; scolding someone; a dress rehearsal for the real thing. *Who are you dressing for?*

dresser   Keeping your drawers tidy; dressing someone down. *Where have you hidden your identity?*

dressing gown   Relaxing; being yourself; feeling vulnerable. *When did you last dress up and go dancing?*

drill   Orderly; boring; repetition; a strong cloth; digging for something; time for the dentist. *Who is acting like a drill sergeant?*

drink   Taking it all in; something fallen into the drink.   *Who is drinking too much?*

drive   Forcing something; working very hard; supplying power; intending; feeling driven; drive-in convenience; a drive-in movie. *What is your dream driving at?*

drive-in   Lazy; convenient; comfortable and private; protected. *When were you last at a drive-in?*

driver   The dream character controlling the action; ambition; boss or father may be indicated; a golf club. *Who is sitting in the driver's seat of your life?*

drop   Time to put it down; let it go; a tiny amount; move when you get the signal; unexpected callers; becoming less; acting at the drop of a hat; a drop-leaf table; only a drop in the bucket; needing more; dropping out of school, or a situation; having the drop on someone; having had a drop too much. *Who has slippery fingers?*

drown   Feeling overwhelmed by emotion; relax; going beyond your limits; feeling like a drowned rat; repressed memories. *What is drowning out your own thoughts?*

drug   Not seeing clearly; addiction; half asleep; check medication. *What acts like a drug in your life?*

drum   Going your own way; supporting a good cause; nervousness; repeating   something; hitting; you have it beaten; drumming up business. *What are you drumming up?*

drumstick   You get the best part; tired of beating your own drum; wanting to be heard. *Who is off the beat?*

drunk   Not being who you really are; taking in stuff that is changing you; overly excited. *When are you out of control?*

dry   A time to rest; don't force the ideas; a sense of humour; feeling dried up; needing more moisturizer; ease up on the drinking. *How has your dream helped you develop more creative ideas?*

duck   Look out; withdraw while you can; something that is real easy for you; not letting it bother you; a strong tape you can use for practically anything.   *What new perspective can you take   so that something doesn't bother you so much?*

duel   Inner conflict; two sides to an issue; witnessing an argument. *Who is challenging you to the end?*

dull   Not clear; insensitive; tiresome; not much energy; needing some quiet time. *What needs sharpening?*

dumb Animal communication; not meeting your expectations; time to exercise; feeling dumbstruck. *What are you afraid of saying?*

dump Drop it off; let go of it; clear out all your cupboards; someone dumping on you; feeling down in the dumps. *What are you feeling gloomy about?*

duplex   Seeing half of the situation; two families or elements involved. *Who do you know who lives or lived in a duplex?*

dusk   That magical time when darkness descends; something to happen just before nightfall. *Who lives in the twilight zone?*

dust   Old and uncared for; not visited for a long time; in need of cleaning; deceiving someone; waiting for the dust to settle. *How have you been hurt or wounded by someone?*

dwarf   A smaller part of yourself; something looming: a magical part of yourself that you keep hidden; your inner critic. *Who are you looking down on?*

dwelling   Where you are; getting stuck on an idea; brooding. *Where is your ideal place to live?*

dye   Changing colours; a part of your life can die and you will be okay; let it go; new life awaits; a   dyed-in-the-wool   type person. *What do you really want to do?*

dynamite   Amazing person; ready to blow up; full of energy. *What explosive situation are you in now?*

"Your dreams are wonderful evidence
of what's going on vibrationally."

Abraham-Hicks

E

when I'd not yet grown
— and still — there are times
flying becomes possible
Nora Leonard

eagle   Needing to achieve greater perspective; soaring and surveying all; keeping an eagle eye on things; United States symbol; spiritual symbol for the soul. *What are your feelings about the dream eagle and what is it saying about your life?*

ear   Paying careful attention; an immature person; not making an impression; dealing with difficulties as they arise; someone is all ears; an ear splitting sound; keeping an ear to the ground; someone wet behind the ears; someone soon to be out on their ear; up to your ears in a situation; someone giving you an earful. *What is going in one ear and out the other?*

earache   Listening more than speaking your own truth; desperate to hear something; working around noise that is too loud. *Who is a pain to listen to?*

early Premature; at the beginning; time is not right yet; early closing or early warning. *What are you always late for?*

earmuffs   Covering up; not listening; not liking what you hear. *What don't you want to hear?*

earring   dressing up for someone; giving someone a telephone call. *Who do you think is talking about you?*

Earth   Mother; basic; foundation; coming down to Earth; earth-shattering news; feeling earthbound. *Who is always practical?*

earthquake Foundations being rocked; check your earthquake provisions; feeling all shook up. *Who has upset your security?*

east   Mysterious; someone or something living east of you; reference to a son. *What new thing is rising in your life?*

Easter   Time to resurrect a valuable part of yourself; re-birth; a new spiritual life. *Who is being crucified?*

eat   Time to nourish yourself; being conscious while you eat; taking back what you said; eating your heart out for someone; check if what you're eating is good for you. *Who has you eating out of their hand?*

echo   Someone repeating you; you repeating yourself; same-o, same-o; what you say reflecting back to you. *Whose voice would you like to hear?*

eclipse   Covering up; loss of importance; failure; something has been made dark. *What large body is covering up your light?*

edge   Extreme; on the brink; disturbed or excited; pushing somebody out; somebody with an advantage; someone uneasy and on edge; time to take the edge off something; trying to get a word in edgewise . *What is setting your teeth on edge?*

education   A time to learn something; remembering times at school. *What do you need to learn now?*

eel   Slippery; electric; shocking; having a hard time holding on. *What is slithering away from you?*

egg   Hiding in a hard shell; new beginning; putting all your hopes in one basket; needing encouragement; being around a bad egg; feeling as if you have egg on your face; egging someone on.   *Who's the egghead?*

eight   Something you ate; an occurrence when you were eight years old; in an awkward position; in numerology eight means material satisfaction. *What special significance does the number eight have for you?*

elastic   Stretching yourself too thin; bouncing back.   *Where in your life could you be more flexible?*

elbow   Playing too much tennis; working hard; cleaning up; a time to bend; too busy; mingling with strange people; seeing the funny side of things. *Who is getting too close to you?*

election   Time to make a choice; democratic decisions. *What do you prefer to do?*

electric   High energy; flowing; going with the current; stimulating; something thrilling. *Who makes your hair stand on end?*

elephant   Carrying a big trunk; a big strong vegetarian; something very large. *What important thing have you forgotten?*

elevator   An up-and-down situation;   feeling enclosed; a funny feeling in your stomach, alerting you to trouble. *What relationship is going up and down?*

eleven   Two ones; a soccer or cricket player; spiritual number related to the Earth's vibration; someone who is eleven; completing things at the eleventh hour, eleven in numerology is a master number and means illumination. *What happened when you were eleven that is relevant to your life now?*

elf   Belief in the unseen world; a special helper; hard-working; a mischievous person. *Who is your favourite elf and why?*

E-mail   A quick answer; instant communication; talking around the world; anonymous friends. *Who do you need to write to?*

embarrassed   Showing off; doing something wrong; shame and regret; afraid of what people think. *What are you too embarrassed to admit?*

embrace   Giving someone a hug; starting a new project; containing and protecting another. *Who do you want to hug?*

embroidery   Fancy talk; traditional women's work; fine crafts; someone having designs on you. *Who is changing the truth to please themselves?*

embryo   An undeveloped state; not yet living independently; protected. *How are you starting all over again?*

emergency   A warning; being too wrought up; look at what needs to be done right now; feeling in a state of emergency. *What have you been putting off?*

emigrate A new place to live; missing your home country. *What part of yourself are you leaving behind?*

emotions A call to action; energy in motion; denying your emotions in waking life. *What is the emotion in your dream guiding you to do?*

employee   A worker; not your own boss; someone else telling you what to do. *Who is not appreciating you?*

employer   Bossy; looking after others; maybe it is time to employ her. (see **boss**) *Where else can you find security?*

employment   Looking for a job; starting something new; start doing it; stop procrastinating. *Who's looking for a job?*

empty   Unloading something; feeling alone; sad; dejected; all gone; going empty-handed; the empty nest syndrome; doing things on an empty stomach. *What part of your life feels empty and how is this dream showing you ways to fill it?*

enchantment   Magic; belief in the metaphysical; someone with great charm. *Who has put a spell on you?*

enclose   Feeling trapped; holding something in; protection; sending something. *What are you holding on to?*

encourage   Needing support; giving someone confidence. *What part of you needs support and inspiration?*

encrypted   Needing to be decoded; hidden; unauthorized access denied. *What are you hiding from others?*

encyclopedia   The quest for knowledge; needing to check out something; looking something up; checking your sources. *What information do you need before acting?*

end   New beginnings waiting; something about to end; someone about to go off the deep end; trying to make ends meet; holding your end up; time to put an end to it; feeling at the end of your tether. *What are you afraid of ending?*

endless   Seems never ending; going on and on and on; something you wished you had never started. *How can you stop it?*

enemy A hostile force showing itself within you; a mental or physical illness; time to take action; refusing to be a victim; being your own worst enemy. *When are you going to forgive them?*

energy   Pep; no energy in waking life; spending a lot of energy and getting nowhere; applying too much force, or not enough. *Where are you sitting on your energy?*

engagement   A joining; going somewhere special; your own engagement. *Who do you know who has recently become engaged and how do they remind you of yourself?*

engine   Power to make things go; check your car engine; time to get things moving. *What is empowering you?*

engraving   A special mark; remembering something; making your mark. *What engraving is important to you?*

enormous   A big deal; feeling overwhelmed; making a big deal out of something. *What small thing are you overlooking?*

enter Going into a new place; beginning; welcomed; showing you the way; perhaps it is time to exit. *What are you about to enter?*

entertain   Give yourself some time off; take a holiday; play; give some thought to a new idea. *When do you act a part to please others and feel too afraid to be completely yourself?*

entrance   A beginning; passing from one phase to another; in a trance; filled with joy and delight. *What does your dream tell you about where to start?*

envelope   A letter given or received; a secret; closed up; surrounded by something. *How are you pushing to new limits?*

epidemic   Passed around from person to person; something moving rapidly; widespread. *What is getting out of control?*

equator   Separating your top half from your bottom; feeling hot around the middle. *Where are you halfway there?*

eruption   Something about to boil over; suppressing your emotions too long. *What are you bursting to say or do?*

escalator   Time to get moving; the ups and downs of life; stairs (stares) that move. *Where or what is the contradiction in your life?*

escape   Needing to get away; not seeing something; watching too much TV. *What are you running away from?*

estate   You are more than you appear to be; exploring parts of yourself; what you own. *What is your present state?*

eucalyptus   Memories of tropical holidays; a clearing out; aromatic bath; clearing out your sinuses; needing to have a good cry; peeling your outer skin. *What rough parts are you getting rid of?*

euchre   Knowing what your partner is going to play; having a trump up your sleeve; something in the cards for you. *How are you outwitting someone?*

evacuate   Clean out; get rid of the garbage and junk; cleanse your body of toxins; time to withdraw. *What do you need to get rid of?*

evergreen   Something that will last through the seasons. *What is it that you want to keep green?*

evil   Living backwards; bad company; someone speaking evil of another; being given the evil eye. *What are you afraid of?*

exaggeration Dreams often exaggerate to get our attention; something in your life taking too much time; blown out of proportion; keep it simple. *What molehill is bothering you?*

examination   Being tested; nervous; afraid of failure; looking carefully. *Where do you feel as if you're under a microscope?*

exchange   Take it back; willing to trade; a fair bargain; second-guessing yourself. *What is it that you wish to change?*

excitement   Life too dull; feelings needed to be stirred up; a high energy level; what excites you is related to your inborn talents. *What do you love to do?*

excrement   Getting rid of waste; not feeling good; taking bad stuff. *How are you allowing yourself to be mistreated?*

execution   Killing off a part of yourself; carrying out a difficult task; finishing something. *What have you not completed?*

executioner   Doing a nasty job; getting rid of unwanted desiring to cut something out of your life. *What are you fed up with?*

exercise   Repeated actions; the need to do something; follow-up; doing what you know is right; getting the right kind of physical exercise. *What needs to be worked out?*

exhibition   A show-off; feeling insecure; being in the public eye. *What happened at the last exhibition you attended?*

exit   The way out; time to leave; someone leaving; finding the exit. *What are you leaving?*

expensive   Not feeling good enough; something too costly for you; rare; precious; having expensive tastes; time to treat yourself. *What is too expensive?*

experiment   Trying something new; plan it out first; a trial. *What are you testing in your life, and is it ethical?*

expert   Feelings of inferiority; needing to take more schooling or training; being the best you can be; calling in the experts for help. *Who's the know-it-all?*

explain   A need to justify; giving too many reasons; wanting to understand; resisting. *What are you trying to explain away?* **explode** Anger; rage; holding it all in; rejecting someone's ideas or theories; out of control. *What is about to explode?*

exploration   Looking at hidden meanings; uncharted country within yourself; seeking new knowledge. *What do you need to look at?*

expose Unprotected; showing how you really feel; feeling vulnerable; (see **naked**) *What are you afraid of exposing?*

expressway   Getting there fast; difficulty in expressing oneself; not having enough exits. *What way-out expression describes you?*

exterior   Inside; on the surface; going by outward appearances. *What are you afraid to show on the outside?*

extraterrestrial   Beyond the ordinary; keeping open to new discoveries; time to phone home. *What do you believe?*

eye   Observing yourself (I); something attracting your attention; believing in an eye for an eye philosophy; a real eye-opener; considering something; refusing to look at something; having your eye on something; not seeing eye-to-eye; can't take your eyes off it; up to your eyeballs in it; getting an eyeful; an eyesore; approaching something with your eyes wide open. *Who is eyeballing you?*

"Dreams are our birthright."

Jill Gregory

F

Fleeting dreams—seeking—
To wake amidst the roaring.
Morning comes too soon.
Gloria Nye

face   Having to face up to what is bothering you; the front of something; facing a person down; having to face someone; losing dignity and self respect; being sad; having to face the facts; someone in your face; putting on a brave face; afraid to show your face; time to appear somewhere important; taking things at face value.   *Who is being two-faced?*

factory Feeling like life's a drudge; boring, repetitive work. *What are you manufacturing or making up?*

fail   Feeling you have not measured up to someone else's standard; warning; time to redefine failure; learning from mistakes; it's just feedback. *How can you change failure into success?*

fair   A fair-haired person; a fair deal; fair play; selling your goods; going to a fair; feeling you are not being treated fairly; paying a fare. *Who is the fair weathered friend?*

fairy tale   Waiting for life to be perfect; the end of the story; life is what you make it; look at the meaning or moral of your dream fairy tale; someone not telling you the truth.   (see **ferry**) *What is your favourite fairy tale and how is your life like it?*

fake   Not being told the truth; fake it till you make it; a counterfeit. *Who is pretending?*

fall   Going down; you can change falling to flying; fear; being the fall guy; temptation; be careful you are not riding for a fall. *Which of the following phrases is your dream alerting you to? Fall across, fall apart, fall away, fall back, fall behind, fall down on, fall flat, fall for, fall from grace, fall heir to, fall in, fall off, fall on, fall out, fall short, fall through, fall under.*

false   Covering up something; pretending to be something you are not; wrong information given; deception; a false start, or false alarm. *Who is being gullible?*

fame   Feeling insignificant; someone doing something conspicuous. *What would you like to be famous for?*

family   Bonded unit; needing support; time to pay attention to someone in your family; memories of early family experiences affecting your life now; studying your family tree. *What group are you involved with that reminds you of your family?*

famous   Wanting attention; wishful thinking; not appreciating what you have. *How are you developing qualities similar to your famous dream character?*

fan   Time to cool off; lots of fans; somebody blowing hot and cold; stirring up something; spreading out; striking out; a fan of someone. *Who is fanning your flame?*

fang   Biting off more than you can chew; a snake in the grass; needing a dental checkup. *Who is being overly defensive?*

farm   Simplify; time to get more experience before you hit the big leagues; eating fresh fruits and vegetables; getting back to basics. *How can you be self-sufficient?*

fat   Needing warmth or protection; feeling insignificant; letting the fat get into the fire; eating the right fats; a fat head; living off the fat of the land. *Who is the weight-watcher?*

father   Dealings with a male authority figure; a need for nurturing; say your prayers; your native country. *Who is like a father to you?*

faucet   going with the flow; turning the flow on and off; a fan of Farrah's. (see **tap**) *Who's the annoying drip?*

fawn   Innocent and helpless; cringing and bowing down to someone. *Who do you call dear?*

fax   A quick message; being electronically scanned; copied and sent on your way; not having all the facts. *What important faxes have you sent, or are waiting for?*

fear   Needing to look at something; life may be too dull; in awe of something. *What have you not been facing in waking life?*

feast   Bountiful gifts coming your way; overeating; too much of a good thing; a gathering of friends; feasting your eyes on something special. *What do you want to celebrate?*

feather   A white feather may signify cowardice; something to be proud of; prayers; a feather-brain in your midst; light and airy; bravery; feathering your nest. *What have you done to earn your feathers?*

feed   Taking care of others; getting enough yourself; needing to get feedback. *What part of yourself are you not feeding?*

fence   A barrier; feeling fenced in or out; having trouble making up your mind; not giving a direct answer; giving clever answers to your opponents. *Where have you but up barriers?*

fender   Protection; guarding you from harm; having to fend for yourself; resisting someone; bumping into an old friend – or enemy. *Who is splashing mud at you?*

fern   Soft;   gentle; a need to be taken care of; Fern; a reminder of Victorian times; absorbing negative energy. *Who likes ferns?*

Ferris wheel   Going around and around and getting nowhere; just swinging in mid-air; going high and getting stuck; wheel of fate. *When were you last at the fair?*

ferry   Using your imagination to see the truth; moving over the unconscious; moving away from being an island; going back and forth and getting nowhere new. (see **fairy**) *Where are you going?*

festival   A time to celebrate; joyous; getting together with friends. *What festive occasion are you planning?*

fetus   New ideas still unborn; new beginnings, lots of feet. *What new project are you bringing into the world?*

fiddle   Fit as a fiddle; someone cheating; playing second fiddle; time on your hands; someone who plays the violin. *What do you have to fiddle with to make it work properly?*

field   Large background for your work; time for harvesting; someone playing the field; check out your field of vision; changing your field of work. *Who is outstanding in their field?*

fight   Too passive in waking life; something bothering you that you need to address; a part of yourself you disagree with; giving it a fighting chance; putting up a fair fight. *Who are you angry with?*

file Getting things in order; sharpen your claws; trim the ends. *What important paper have you misplaced?*

filing cabinet   Keeping old thoughts filed away for too long; storing important and private documents; holding on to things. *What are you holding on to that you no longer need?*

film A need to record something; looking back at old photos; learning from movies; a movie buff. *What are you covering up with a thin layer?*

find   Needing   more information; someone has lost something precious; finding something at last; finding your way; a real find. *What are you looking for?*

finger   Telling on someone; letting it slip away; working your fingers to the bone; wanting to have a finger in the pie; count on the fingers of one hand;   index finger—pointing to something, making a point; middle finger—anger and sexuality, giving someone the finger;   ring finger—marriage or engagement, love; baby finger—heart related, a young self;   being twisted around someone's little finger. thumb— putting your thumb on it and a green thumb. *Who or what is your dream finger point out?*

fire   Things getting hot; angry but afraid to show it; meddling with something dangerous; under attack or blame; getting all fired up about a new project; afraid of being fired; passion and sexual love; impatience. *Who is trying to set the world on fire?*

firecracker   Feeling ready to explode; time to celebrate; an excited person. *Who do you want to light your fire?*

fire escape   Getting out of a hot situation; planning a safety route; running from the heat. *What, or who, is too hot to handle?*

firefighter   Fighting fire with fire; lots of anger; hot people around you; trying to cool things down; being embroiled in a hot issue. *What, or who, are you trying to cool down?*

first   Feeling as if you always come in last; having first hand knowledge; needing to put first things first; wanting to be first; going first class. *What's the first thing you need to do?*

fish   Emotions or the unconscious; feeling uncomfortable in your environment; a person born under the sign of Pisces; looking for compliments; something fishy going on; drinking like a fish; an early secret sign meaning Jesus; realizing there are plenty of fish in the sea. *Who's the cold fish?*

fist   Wanting to pick a fight; unable to receive; holding on too tightly. *Who is being aggressive?*

five   A full hand; a friendly wave; the Pentagon; a five o'clock shadow; in numerology five stands for constructive freedom; making a list; someone being a handful; five of something.   *What are you rejoicing over?*

flag   Love of country; tired out; white flag—surrender; red flag—tempting or challenging something to attack you; black flag—pirating; feeling flagged and exhausted; flagging someone down. *What new ideas have you presented?*

flat   Feeling low; depressed; everything going smoothly; final say on something; going at maximum speed; having no effect at all; feeling like flattening someone; falling flat on your face. *Who do you know who lives in a flat (apartment)?*

flea   Picky, picky details that are driving you crazy; a tiny matter bugging you; someone is a parasite; going to a flea market for bargains. *What are you itching to do?*

float   Not a care in the world; sailing over top; time to dive in; trust; moving effortlessly. *What or who are you avoiding?*

flood   Feeling overwhelmed;   there is no end to the ideas you have; time for the floodgates to open; wanting to be in the floodlights. *What is about to overflow?*

floor   Check out what is supporting you; someone else has the floor and is calling the shots. *What has recently floored you?*

flour   Buy yourself some flowers; baking up some new ideas. (see **flower**) *What's rising to the surface?*

flow   Go with it and life will be easier; a flow of ideas or action; a flow charts. *What has stopped moving easily for you?*

flower   Beauty around you that you might not be noticing; look at aroma therapy for health issues; someone who speaks
in flowery language; flower power. (see **flour**) *What is about to come into full flower?*

flute   There is a little of Pan in all of us; dance and be happy. *Who do you know who plays the flute?*

fly   A symbol that you are in alignment with your higher/inner self; freedom of expression; doing the impossible; creativity and getting a broader perspective; your body doesn't have to keep you down; moving to great heights; soaring above the crowd; a new freedom; attacking someone; leaving suddenly; getting very excited; take good aim and let go; a fancy fish hook; there are no flies on you; a fly-by-night character. *What or who is the fly in the ointment that threatens to spoil things?*

flying saucer   Feeling like throwing plates at someone; things flying around you that you can't identify. *What is alien in your life?*

fog   Getting a clear picture of what you are doing; things not clear. confused and puzzled; a Mel Torme fan. *Who is in a fog?*

foil   Stopped; getting the better of someone; protecting something you are cooking up; a fencing partner; someone who is your opposite making you look great. *What in your life looks better by contrast?*

food   Nurturing; being looked after; eating too much, or not enough. *What are you missing in your life?*

fool   Wisdom in disguise; a silly person around you; still amusing the king; wasting time; foolhardy; being nobody's fool. *Who has been tricked?*

foot   The bottom of an issue; holding something up; the end of it; get walking; putting your best foot forward; putting your foot down; putting your foot in it; someone underfoot; an old person ready to pass over; someone with feet of clay; getting your feet wet; having both feet on the ground; getting your foot in the door. *What is 12 inches long?*

football   Score a touchdown; run like crazy; catch what's coming to you; keep your eye on the ball. *Who is the man in tight pants?*

foreign country   A strange place; looking at the situation with new eyes. *What is feeling foreign or unfamiliar to you?*

forest   Getting lost in the details and not seeing the whole; identifying with Robin Hood; hiding out; looking at life as if it were a box of chocolates. *What can't you find your way out of?*

forget   Letting it go; making a list. *What have you forgotten?*

forgive   Letting go of the past; needing to express the anger and hurt before you can forgive. *Who do you need to forgive?*

fork   Time to make a decision; left or right; waiting; time to hand it over; pitching something; lifting something heavy. *Where in your life are you at a fork in the road?*

formal   Stiff and uncomfortable; too concerned with the form and not the content; all dressed up and nowhere to go. *Where in your life are you being too conventional?*

fort   Heavily protected; unable to get through; armed and ready. *What are you hiding behind for protection?*

fortune cookie   Contained; a message comes to you in a strange way; Chinese. *What are you hoping to find?*

fossil   Unearthing old forms; stuck in your ways; feeling petrified. *What old stuff are you digging up?*

fountain   Flowing; the unconscious; on-again, off-again with your emotions; look to the original source. *Which fountain are you looking for—youth or knowledge?*

four   Symbol of wholeness; four seasons; four elements - fire, earth, water, air; the most common number appearing in dreams; one for each corner; balanced; on hands and knees; bluffing; a four-flusher; a person who uses four-letter words; a four-wheel drive; in numerology four stands for order and service. *What is it for?*

fox   Sly; careful; playing dumb; melting into your surroundings; hiding in your foxhole; dancing the fox trot; planning your next move well. *Who is the fox that you want to date?*

frame   Surrounded; having an outline; supporting structure; made to feel guilty. *What thought needs reframing?*

free   Feeling trapped; needing to get away; confirming the right action; freedom to, or freedom from; without cost; not following any rules; using something as if it were your own. *What do you need to set free in yourself?*

freeze   A cold person; someone giving you the cold shoulder; holding on too tightly; excluding someone; doing some fancy decorating; freezing up. *What part of you is frozen or feels numb?*

freight   Feeling like extra baggage; carrying a weight; delivering something. *What are you lugging around that could be unloaded?*

fridge   Putting your plans in cold storage; keeping things fresh. *Who's turned off?*

friend   A person similar to you; a helpful part of yourself; phone your friend; an enemy in disguise. *Who is there to help you?*

frightening   Needing a jolt of energy; afraid of something; life may be too dull; suppressing your fears and acting brave. *What does the frightening part of the dream remind you of?*

frog A hope for the future; comfortable in two mediums; hopping along; someone who speaks as if they have a frog in their throat. *Have you found your prince yet?*

front A beginning; in the front lines; a cover-up; someone before you. *Who is putting on a front?*

frost Acting cool; holding your emotions in check; something frosted over. *What do the pictures on the windows suggest?*

frozen Time to thaw out; frozen emotions; feeling unable to move; scared. (see **defrost**) *What needs to be thawed out?*

fruit More sweetness needed; something is coming to fruition; full and juicy; a nutty person. *What is about to bear fruit?*

frying pan Something getting hot; feeling burned or cheated; eating too many fried foods. *Have you just jumped out of it, or into it?*

fudge There are no calories in dream fudge; give yourself some rewards. *What are you faking?*

fugitive Running away from something; fleeting; hard to catch; loss of identity. *What are you chasing after, or running from?*

full Overflowing; no more room; absorbed; come full circle; full steam ahead; coming to a full stop; in full swing; in full view; on a full stomach; a full moon. *What is empty that you want to fill up?*

fun Time to relax and play; not having enough fun; poking fun at someone; providing amusement for others. *What isn't fun anymore?*

funeral Time to bury the past; fear of dying; memory of a funeral; getting into a heap of trouble. *Who do you need to say goodbye to?*

furious   A serious loss; time to show your true feelings. *Who are you so mad at?*

furnace   Things heating up; holding your anger in. *Who is hot under the collar?*

furniture   Parts of yourself; moving things around; getting stuck in one place; replacing something; feeling like part of the furniture. *What new furniture do you want or need?*

fuse   Someone with a short fuse; protection when things get too hot; melt together; blending things. *What is about to blow up and how can you protect yourself?*

future   A possibility; having high hopes; buying stuff now to be sold later; wondering what is going to happen. *What plans do you need to make?*

"There is no wrong way to dream."

Joan Duncan

G

—flow of poetry
I wake in the night to net
the fleeting haiku
Nora Leonard

gag   Being stopped from talking; closed up; a joke; choking on something that is hard to swallow. *Who is the butt of the joke?*

galaxy   Somebody who is way out there; all over the place; needing more space; a brilliant mass of stars; something huge; movie lover. *What do you want to get away from?*

gallery Showing what you can do; exposing your creativity; watching from on high. *Who are you trying to please?*

gallop   Running away from something; in a hurry; flying through the air; horses. *What's the big hurry?*

gallows   Feeling hung over; afraid of losing your neck; just hanging around. *What are you feeling guilty about?*

gamble   Taking a risk; an addiction;   fear of losing something.   *What past gambles have paid off?*

game   Time to play; don't take life so seriously; you are ahead of the game; following the rules. *What life games are you playing?*

gang   Time to phone up your old pals; being picked on; too many people around you; feeling ganged up on. *Which gang's all here?*

gangrene   Something needing attention; feeling rotten. *What part of you are you ready to let go?*

gangster   Feeling victimized; somebody telling you what to do; a need for some excitement and adventure in your life. *Who do you know who acts like a gangster?*

garage   Time to get rid of stuff; look at what you have stored away; look after your body. *What's in your garage?*

garbage   Old stuff to discard; look at who you treat like garbage; clean out things. *Who is handing you a line of garbage?*

garbage can   Getting rid of what is no longer useful; feeling unable to deal with all the garbage in your life. *What are you afraid to throw out?*

garden   A time for growth and nurturing; pull out the weeds that are choking you; look after the details every day. *What is flowering in your life?*

gardenia   Sweet-smelling; romantic. *Where is your secret garden?*

gargoyle Scary creatures around you; protection. *Who's there just hanging around, looking like a monster?*

garlic   Purifying the blood; peeling away layers; protective powers. *Who are you trying to keep away?*

garter   Something constricting your movement; sexy thoughts; the next fellow to be married; a night from long ago. *Who's the old fashioned gal?*

gas   Too many beans; boastful; a time for laughter. *Who is full of hot air?*

gasoline   Fuel for the journey; an explosive situation; *What energizes you?*

gate A way through; a passage; an opening; a new opportunity. *Who would you like to give the gate to?*

gather   Joining together; bring things around you that you need. *What are you looking for?*

gauge   Measuring; check your meters. *Whose reactions are you constantly monitoring for approval?*

gauntlet   Going through a particularly trying time; feeling pressured to perform; others judging you. *What action are you determined to carry out, despite danger threatening from all sides?*

gauze   Covering up old wounds; flimsy and unsupported; airy-fairy. *How have you been a mummy too long?*

gavel   Trying to get someone's attention; no one listens to you; laying down the law. *Who needs discipline?*

gay   Old-fashioned happiness; dealings with someone of the same sex; looking at the opposite gender within yourself. *What gay person has influenced you?*

gazebo   A romantic garden shelter; a secret tryst. *Who would you like to meet in a summer house?*

gazelle   Light of foot; soft eyes. *Who do you know who is fast, graceful and shy?*

gear   Get into the right speed; clashing as you change speeds; in gear. *Where have you left all your stuff?*

gecko   Good luck, especially if one falls on your head; ready to climb the walls. *Who is the friendly little creature around you?*

geisha   Disciplined; witty and entertaining; serving; party-goer. *Who is tired of fulfilling another's desires?*

gem   Your special gifts; something precious to be found; be grateful for what you have. *Who is the gem in your life?*

general   Being bossed around; vague; unsure; not too good at following orders. *What is generally bothering you right now?*

genie   Jeannie or Gene; a magical person; being impractical; hoping that magic will solve the problem, a belief in the unexpected. *What are your three wishes?*

genius   Feeling inferior; having some great ideas, but not knowing what to do with them; over-inflated opinion. *What genius thought up the latest problem you are in?*

gentleman   a male caller; a man who needs to be more gentle; refined; a model for you; a polite group of men. *Who needs to improve their manners?*

geodesic dome Breaking out of a mold; the square is too sharp for you; curved energy is needed. *Where is the dome?*

geography   Feeling part of the Earth; living where you want to; hills and valleys. *Where on Earth do you think you're going?*

geometry   Points, lines, surfaces, solids; visualizing in three dimensions. *What is steadily progressing for you?*

geranium   Living in a window box; cheerful, but stuck. *Who do you know who loves geraniums?*

gerbil   On a treadmill you can't seem to get off; living in a cage; warm and fuzzy. *Who owns a gerbil?*

germ   Fear of disease; full of new ideas; the beginning of something. *What little things are bugging you?*

gesture   Show what you mean with actions rather than words; look at what people are saying with their bodies; a hollow offering. *Who is rude, but speaking so sweetly?*

ghost   Belief in the unseen; writing for someone else; a slight suggestion; pale. *Who has passed on who you would like to talk to?*

ghoul   Wanting to have a good scare; someone creepy around you; someone feeding on the energy of others. *What would you like to say to that old ghoul?*

giant   Feeling small and insignificant; a tall, imposing person in your life; feelings overwhelming you; parental authority, particularly the father. *What is being blown out of proportion?*

gift   Being given something of value; giving; birthday coming up; a gift of the gab. *What gift has this dream given you?*

gig   Playing around; a musician in your midst; the gig is up. *What gig would you like to play?*

giggle   Silly; not to be taken seriously; have a little fun; childlike. *What can you release with a good giggle?*

gill   A cold fish; swimming upstream; trapped by your breath; someone named Gill or Gillian. *Who is having trouble breathing?*

gilt   Bright covering; royalty; ornaments; all that glitters is not gold. (see **guilt**) *What beauty are you not appreciating?*

gin   English person; time to relax; maybe you need a tonic. *Who's the card shark?*

ginger   Women's issues; a pet or   person named Ginger; hot and spicy; full of energy. *Who is sugar and spice and everything nice?*

gingham   A country lass; plain and simple.   *What do you need to check out?*

giraffe   Sticking your neck out; a lot to swallow; a sore neck; swift but silent; a tall story; long reach. *Whose head is in the clouds?*

girdle   Feeling restricted; difficulty in taking a deep breath; changing yourself to please others; encircled. *What are you holding in?*

girl   You can do and be what you want to; look at what was happening in your life when you were the age of the girl in the dream. *Who is a grown woman and still being called a girl?*

glacier   A large cold mass in your life; slow-moving; taking a long time to thaw out. *What large mountain are you coming down from?*

glamorous   Wanting to please; feeling insecure; sexy; playing a game; enchanting others. *Who is clamouring to be glamorous?*

glass See through; shine up the surface; feeling exposed; no place to hide; seeing through rose-coloured glasses. *What is being reflected to you?*

glaze Not fully conscious; half-awake; covering up mistakes; watered down. *What are you glazing over, and hoping it won't show through?*

glide Easy; smooth going; on the right track; a graceful landing. *What has started to smooth out for you?*

glitter All show; nothing underneath; sparkling to get your attention. *What is pretending to be precious?*

globe Emblem of power; symbolism of totality; in Christian iconography – the whole thing; holding the world in your hands; going on a long journey; sphere-shaped. *Who is the globe trotter?*

glockenspiel The bells toll for you; making happy music; Germany/ Austria. *For what are you being summoned?*

glossary Get the words straight; be sure you know the terms of the deal; new expressions. *What parts don't you understand?*

glove The executive hand; a pledge of action: white gloves symbolize purity; removing the right glove acknowledged the superiority of an overlord or sovereign; giving someone a hand; a challenge; using your hands; a perfect fit; ready for a fight. *Who are you handling with kid gloves?*

glue Feeling stuck; someone stuck up; can't get away. *What do you have your eyes, or attention, glued to?*

glutton Wanting it all; eating too much food; undernourished. *Who isn't getting enough?*

gnat   Nat; some little nuisance around you. *Who is taking little bites out of you?*

gnome   A mischievous part of you has a message, believe the unbelievable; guarding the treasures you keep underground. (see **elf**) *Who is the odd, little person you know?*

goal   Re-evaluate your goals; time to set some goals; scoring; guarding the net; being driven. *What goal is not worth the price?*

goat   Goat cheese; an old goat; a person with their sun sign in Capricorn; being a scapegoat and taking all the blame; virility or lust in the male; nourishing in the female; in China goat and yang are homonyms and goat is a positive masculine symbol. *Who is getting your goat?*

goblet   Wine of life; drinking something in; Holy Grail; special spiritual significance symbolizing the Last Supper. *What special message is being passed to you in this dream?*

goblin   Scary little thoughts; Hallowe'en and harvest time; trick-or-treat. *Who has been acting like a mischievous elf lately?*

god   A know-it-all; look at what you have made into a god in your life. *Who are you treating like a god?*

God   A BIG dream; connecting to Source; feeling looked after and protected. *What did God communicate to you?*

goggle can't believe what you have just seen; look carefully; protect your eyes; going skiing or snorkeling. *What are you afraid of seeing?*

gold The sun; transformation; earthly powers; spirit of enlightenment; a masculine symbol; precious and wonderful thoughts or intuitions;

discovering treasures; valuable findings; digging for financial freedom. *What do you value most?*

goldfish Swimming with wealth; your emotions hold treasures; feeling watched. *What is the gold in your life?*

golf Place to make contacts; a lot of walking and hitting things; needing more exercise. *What are you driving at?*

gondola Trip to Venice; being taken for a ride; keeping score. *Who is paddling your boat?*

gong A signal; a warning; having dinner prepared for you. *What important item have you forgotten?*

goose A lot of honking over nothing; getting goose-bumps; migration south; frightened; sacrificing long-term advantage for short-term gain. *Whose goose has been cooked?*

gopher Running errands; hiding in a hole and only popping up to see what's happening. *What is it that you have to go for?*

gorilla Large, fierce, powerful; jungle mentality; animal origins. *Who's the Neanderthal?*

gossip Telling tales out of school; keep others' secrets to yourself. *What are you afraid that people are saying about you?*

gourd Feeling dried up and hollowed out; a container; not having it all together; autumn. *What are you trying to hold together?*

government Authority figure; being told what to do; not feeling free; pressure; a need to govern yourself. *What dealings have you had with the government that are a challenge to you?*

gown Feeling underdressed; all dressed up and no place to go; a member of the university; a nightgown. *When do you wear a gown?*

graduate Congratulations, you made it; remember your own graduation; making the grade; something gradually changing. *What are you nearing completion?*

grail Special container; looking for something to fulfil you.(see **Holy Grail**) *What are you longing to drink in?*

grain Eating grains; looking only at the surface; the quality of something, a food sensitivity. *What is rubbing you the wrong way?*

grandchild A young and special person; a younger version of yourself. *Who is the terrific kid you know?*

grandparent A wise part of yourself; being a great parent. *What advice could you seek from an older, wiser person?*

grapes Fine wines; the good things in life; sweet and nurturing; the nectar of the gods; a wino, sour grapes. *What news is going through the grapevine?*

grapefruit Grapes and fruits; breakfast foods; something round and juicy; healthy eating. *Who wants to lose weight?*

graph Seeing it in black and white; make a chart; something scaled-down. *What picture are you not seeing clearly?*

grasp Holding on too tightly; let it go; eagerly accepting; understanding something. *What are you afraid of losing?*

grass Smoking pot; wasting time by letting the grass grow under your feet; needing to eat more greens. *Whose grass do you perceive as greener than yours – and is it really?*

grasshopper Playing in the grass; a hop-head. *Who are you trying to get the jump on?*

grate Grating on your nerves; behind bars; grinding or wearing you down. *What is really great in your life?*

grateful Noticing what's good; feeling great; not recognizing someone. *Who is not grateful?*

grave Fear of death; serious; digging yourself a hole; remembering someone who has died. *Who have you made "turn in their grave"?*

gravel A bumpy path; check your kidneys; a raspy voice. *Where do you travel on a country road?*

gravestone Marking a serious item; remembering someone who has died; something written that cannot be changed. *What would you like your epitaph to be?*

graveyard Peaceful and at rest; a serious yard at your house; visiting those who have passed; burying something forever. *Who works the graveyard shift?*

gravy Time for special things; easy gain or profit; having to eat a bland diet. *Who do you resent who is on a gravy train?*

grease Slippery; fat; getting burned. *Who is the unctuous, disagreeable person with whom you have to deal?*

greed   Wanting more than a fair share; a belief in scarcity; unwillingness to share. *What don't you have enough of?*

green   Back to Earth; eat more greens; healing; money concerns; a green light to go ahead with your plans; someone without experience. *Who are you envious of, or is envious of you?*

gremlin   Someone getting in your way; a nuisance. *What are you blaming on the gremlins?*

grenade Eating too many pineapples; making an irreversible decision; a bomb being dropped. *What is too hot to handle?*

greyhound Taking a bus trip; sleek and fast; slim of body; being hounded by a grey-haired person. *What are you racing to?*

griddle   Someone in a flap; sizzling affair.   *Whose has had their bacon cooked?*

grief   Expressing sorrow; getting stuck in the past; forgetting the good parts. *Who are you still mourning?*

grill   In the hot seat; fast and cheap.   *Who is grilling you?*

grind Worn down; drinking too much coffee; studying long hours. *Who is keeping their nose to the grindstone?*

grip Hanging on tightly; time to come to grips with something; losing control; packing thoughts away. *Who needs to get a grip?*

grizzly bear   Feeling threatened and endangered; old and gray; helpless; someone bad tempered; needing to bear up. *Who's the bear in your life?*

grocery store   Needing nourishment; having a selection;. *Who is buying gross stuff?*

groom   New beginnings; making yourself presentable. (see **bridegroom**) *Who is the lucky guy?*

groove   Stuck in the same old rut; going around and around and getting nowhere; musical. *Who is in the groove?*

ground   Foundation; feeling safe; grounded and centered; squished into little bits; beginning to build something new; go the distance; going forward; holding your position. *What is grinding you down?*

groundhog   Using too much space;   needing six more weeks of preparation; afraid of your own shadow. *Who is the prairie dog?*

group   Alone too much; not asking for help; group consensus. *Who hates joining groups?*

grow   Confirmation that you are growing; maturing; developing; something getting bigger. *What is having an increasing effect on you?*

growl   Not pleased; complaining; angry; grumpy and unsociable; hungry. *Who is making all the noise?*

grown   Full height; finished sprouting; a time to grow. *Who is all grown up?*

grub   Eating the wrong kinds of food; digging for something; beginning a new project. *Who is the slimy character in your life?*

grudge   Feeling resentful; begrudging someone something; a long-standing dislike. *Who do you have a grudge against?*

guard   Feeling in need of protection;   watching over something; feeling unprepared. *Who has their guard up?*

guess   Not having all the facts; name-brands only. *How can you take the guess work out of the situation?*

guest   Unexpected company; feeling not part of the family; making special preparations. *Who has overstayed their welcome?*

guide   Something to show you the way; in need of guidance; a special guide for you. *What has your dream guided you to do?*

guillotine   Thoughts and feelings separated; cutting up important papers. *What, or who, have you lost your head over?*

guilt   Feeling bad about something;   taking on someone else's guilt; being made to feel guilty when you are not. *What are you blaming yourself for now?*

guinea pig   A pig being tested; treated as an experiment; needing to be taken care of. *What new things are you trying out?*

guitar   Making sweet music; strumming along; being strung along. *Who do you know who plays the guitar?*

gulf   A wide space between you and a loved one; feeling swallowed up by something. *What has caused this gulf between you?*

gull   Feeling free, or the need to be free; living near water. *Where would you like to fly?*

gum   Chewing over ideas; messing things up; a sticky situation; doing some detective work; tasteless. *Who chews gum a lot?*

gun An explosive statement; wanting to injure or kill off something; fear of death; protection; getting an early start; sticking to your guns. *Who is under the gun?*

gush Pouring forth; somebody talking too much and saying nothing. *Who is being false with their praise?*

"It is not unusual for an older figure,
invented by the dreamer,
to do or say something reassuring,
personifying the dreamer's innate wisdom
which goes far beyond her/his years."

Donald Broadribb

Each the fated — each the godly
each the dreamer of this dream
for you are fresh forever's flowing
carried by time's ceaseless stream

Jan. 12, 1987

Ruth Cunningham

H

hidden treasure troves
locked in dream basements,
burning in phantom fires
Nora Leonard

hacksaw   Fierce detachment; abrupt goodbye. What *part of yourself are you trying to hack off?*

hag   Feeling worn out; a vicious old woman. *Who is nagging who?*

hail   Calling forth; hard little things raining on you from above. *What is relevant about where you come from?*

hair   Thoughts; new thoughts growing; untangling thoughts; tying your thoughts up in knots; smoothing them out; someone getting in your hair; time to let your hair down. *How are you splitting hairs with people?*

hairbrush   Smooth out your thoughts; brush some unimportant thoughts away. *Who is giving you the brush off?*

hairdresser   Time to clean up your thoughts; get new *What's the big secret that only your hairdresser knows?*

hairpin   Makeshift key; pinning down your thoughts; a sharp curve. *Who is sticking pins in your thoughts?*

half   Not getting your full share; something half completed; look to your better half for support. *Who do you need to share with?*

hall   Pulling a big load; in a passage between two places; left outside. *What are you moving between?*

Hallowe'en   Some scary people around you; being given sweets. *Who is pretending to be someone or something they are not?*

halo Spiritual thoughts; a devil in disguise; a special energy surrounding someone. *Who is acting like an angel?*

ham   Eating high on the hog; communication over the air waves. *Who is always hamming it up?*

hammer Time to repair something; going at it with hammer and tongs; beating something into shape. *What are you hammering away at and getting little or no results?*

hammock Get away from it all; take a long lazy holiday; swinging. *Who is the lazy bum?*

hamper Someone short of food; time to clean up your identity; household chores. *What is stopping you from moving forward?*

hamster   Often a first pet; running on a treadmill; feeling caged. *When do you feel warm and fuzzy and looked after?*

hand   Lending a hand; being able to accomplish what you set out to do; doing handiwork or handicrafts; giving compliments; first hand knowledge; spending everything you receive; close relation with someone; having your hands full; consider the other viewpoint; wash your hands of a situation; your hands feel tied; close by. *Who do you have eating out of your hand?*

handbag Your identity; losing/finding your identity; keeping all your stuff together; protect your abilities. *Who is going on a trip?*

handcuff   Feeling trapped; being stopped from doing what you really want to do; hitting someone with your hand, or being hit. *Who or what is holding you back?*

handicap   some part not working up to par; feeling less than; a cap you keep handy; association with golf. *How are you handicapped?*

handkerchief   Feeling sad; old fashioned; using things from the past; nosey. *Who carries a handkerchief?*

handle   Opening something you have been wanting; get a new slant on it; finally grasping what they mean; confirmation that you can handle it okay. *Who flies off the handle?*

handlebars   To get or have a strong handle on; steering; bicycle; sitting precariously. *Who is being the daredevil?*

hang   Just hanging around; getting the hang of something; putting something up and out of your way; hanging back from doing something you want to do; hanging onto something too tightly. *What are you finally getting the hang of?*

hanger   A hanger on; a woman you feel like hanging. *What are you hanging your hopes on?*

harbour   A safe place to go; feeling protected; coming home; getting ready to go on an ocean cruise. *What unnecessary thoughts are you harbouring?*

hardware   Wearing a hard mask; getting a new computer; hanging out in hardware stores. *What is so hard to wear?*

harm   Feeling damaged; being hurt. *What is harming you?*

harmonica   Making playful music; feeling in tune. *Who do you know who plays a mouth organ?*

harness   Feeling held back; all laced up; trapped; working like a horse. *What familiar thing have you recently returned to?*

harp   Continually yakking about something; time to let it go; angel music. *What would be heavenly music to your ears?*

harpoon   New idea; stuck or struck; feeling attacked. *How have you been cruelly struck down?*

harvest   Receiving rewards of your hard work; late summer/ early fall; the consequence of your actions. *What are you thankful for?*

hat   To top it all off; covering up or hiding your thoughts; time to pass the hat; someone talking through their hat; throw your hat into the ring. *What thoughts are you keeping under your hat?*

hatch   New ideas coming forth; breaking out of your shell; a trap door; a way out. *What fine lines are being engraved?*

hate   A love-hate relationship; anger and fear; resistance. *What , or who, do you hate so much, yet can't let go?*

haunt   Recurring thoughts or feelings; a visit to the old place. *What reminds you of your favourite haunt?*

hawk   Circling and looking for prey; something being hawked (sold); a hawk-eyed person. *What are you watching for so intently?*

hay   Calling someone; trying to get somebody's attention; money issues; time to hit the hay. *Who's intent on making hay while the sun shines?*

head   Thoughts; in one's head, detached from feelings; the one in command; keep your head up; something has gone to someone's head; a situation over your head; hiding your head in shame; talking one's head off; something to turn your head; be ready to head off something. *What is coming to a head?*

headlight   Bright ideas; you need some more light on the subject. *Whose eyes need checking?*

headline   Topping the show; newsworthy; worry lines in the forehead. wanting attention. *What is your favourite headline?*

heal   Walking a lot; feeling run down; someone not following orders; a return to health. (see **heel**) *Who's the heel?*

health   Health issues; drinking to your health; doing what's good for you. *What health challenge are you facing that your dream could be helping you with?*

heart   Love; heartache; something after your own heart; doing kind things for others because your heart is in the right place; someone with a heart of gold; wearing your heart on your sleeve; do it with all your heart. *Who are you missing?*

hearth   Warm and cozy; being looked after; home; family. *What are you longing for?*

heaven   Spiritual thoughts; attempting to move heaven and earth; stargazing. *What in heaven's name are you doing?*

heavy   Dark thoughts; a heavy handed person around; something hanging heavy over you; needing lifting up; heavy duty; stop playing the heavy. *What heavy load are you carrying for someone else?*

hedge   Separation; being hemmed in; a hedgehog; evading something. *Who is hedging their bets?*

heel   Healing; someone close by you; time to cool your heels; feeling down at the heels; take to your heels and run; a vulnerable part.   (see **heal**)   *In what project are you dragging your heels?*

heir/heiress   Being left something of importance; responsibility for what others have left. *What are the gifts of your ancestors?*

heirloom   A precious memento from a family member; remember the past. *What story has been woven on your family loom?*

helicopter   Whirling around in one place; going up and down; making a landing in tight places; being rescued. *Who do you want to get away from quickly?*

hell   Things are getting hot; feeling guilty; prolonged suffering about to end; something about to break loose. *What feels like hell?*

helmet   Heavily protecting thoughts; keeping your thoughts encased; meeting something hellish. *What thoughts don't you want to leak out?*

help   Helping too much; needing help; time to help yourself.   *Who needs helping?*

helpless   feeling victimized; experiencing the other side; perhaps it is time to help less. *Who is being helpless?*

hem Something is going to turn up; hesitating about doing something; afraid to say something; needing someone's attention. *What are you wearing that is dragging you down?*

hen   Preparing to hatch something; not comfortable in the pecking order. *Who is acting like a mother hen?*

herb   Alternative healing methods; a person named Herb. *What herbs would be good for you right now?*

herd   Going along with the crowd; too many people around you. *What have you heard lately that you would rather not have?*

hermit   Living alone too much; keeping to yourself; come out of your cave and share your knowledge; a crabby person living in a portable shelter. *Who do you know is living like a hermit?*

hero/heroine   Wanting someone to rescue you; needing to be regarded as a rescuer; acting beyond the call of duty; addicted to heroin. *Who is your personal heroine?*

hexagon   The hex has gone; six of something; six tries. *What in your life is a hexagon shape?*

hibernate   Time to rest and recoup; slow down your activity; living with a bear. *Who haven't you seen for a while?*

hide   Someone after your hide; feeling threatened; protect your skin. *What are you hiding?*

hieroglyphic   Picture writing; realizing what the pictures mean; something important that is difficult to read. *What mystery do you need to figure out?*

high   An expansive view; seeing things from another perspective; feeling low; greeting friends; flying high; left high and dry without help. *Who is acting high and mighty?*

high school   Having a high opinion of school; saying hello to new learning; remembering your high school years. *What happened in high school that is similar to what is happening now?*

hike   Needing to walk more; a long hike to where you want to get; a raise in pay. *Who would you like to tell to take a hike?*

hill   Looking up to higher things or if you are on the top, looking down; check out the ants and moles around you making hills. *Who is heaping up the dirt around you?*

hinge   Bending back and forth; possible problems with your elbows or knees. *What is hinging on your action?*

hip   With it; up to date; a cheer for you; be careful of your hips; rose hip tea. *Who is quick to draw from the hip?*

hippopotamus   Animals often mean instincts; these would be very large and slow moving instincts. *What's the big problem that feels as if it weighs four tons?*

history   Related to something in the past; look back over recent history for a clue; you are about to make history. *What is it about his story that alarmed you?*

hit   Right on; hitting or being hit; anger; aggressiveness; hitting below the belt; hitting it off: a project that is hit or miss. *Where in your dream or your life have you hit the nail on the head?*

hitch   Joining; coming together; a possible marriage; being caught; things going smoothly without a hitch; be careful of hitchhikers. *What's the hitch?*

hive   A busy household; someone acting like a queen bee; lots of buzzing around; stressed out and getting hives. *Who is in the middle of a hive of activity?*

hockey   Fighting instead of playing; someone hawking or hocking a key; a hawk is the key; the key is to get out of hock, keeping score; setting goals. *What is the significance of hockey in your life?*

hoe   Getting rid of weeds and old thoughts that are growing out of control; telling you to laugh more. *How can you loosen up those feelings of being buried?*

hog   Not getting enough; someone hogging it all; having the best of everything; go the whole hog. *What have you been hogging that you need to share?*

hold   Hanging on; in storage; waiting for the right moment; stop holding back; holding your own position; hold out for what you really want; feeling held up. *What are you holding onto too tightly?*

hole   Seeing the whole; unified; an empty place; burning a hole in your pocket; in debt; time to hole up for a while; a hole in one. *Who is picking holes in your plan and what can you do about it?*

holiday   Needing some time off; lighten up; working too hard; *What is special about this holiday?*

hollow An empty place inside you; feeling empty.   *Who is making hollow promises?*

holly   A Christmas memory; a woman named Holly. *What do holly boughs mean to you?*

Hollywood   Feeling insecure; a desire for fame; connection with the movies. *Who would you like to visit in Hollywood?*

holster   Being prepared; put your guns away. *Who is trying to shoot you down?*

holy   A spiritual dream; a connection to the Divine Source; feeling whole. *Whose plan is full of holes?*

home   Feeling homesick; needing comfort; memories of a home. *What makes you feel at home?*

homosexual   A message to love yourself; seeing yourself in others of the same sex; a challenge to look at basic beliefs; acceptance of those who have different lifestyles; risking others disapproval; courage. *What do you love most about yourself?*

honey   Being too sweet and nice; a honey of a deal, a busy bee. *Who do you call honey, or who would you like to call honey?*

honk   Time to fly south; look out; letting people know you are coming through, time to get your ducks and geese in order. *Who is trying to get all the attention?*

hood   Cover up; acting like a criminal; university honours; covering the engine or source of power. *Who's trying to hoodwink you?*

hoof   Sore feet; walking too much; a professional dancer. *Who is kicking you around?*

hook   A way to get people's attention; feeling caught; time to hang something up; getting something by hook or by crook; getting off the hook; doing it on your own. *Who do you want to hook up with?*

hoop   Something that is all around you; hiding under big skirts. *Who are you jumping through hoops for?*

hop   Off balance; having to act immediately; beer drinking; departing quickly. *What project are you ready to hop into?*

hopscotch   Drinking too much beer and scotch; a few more jumps and you're home. *Who is playing childish games with you?*

horizon   Something far off in the distance; looking way out there. *What is coming up on the horizon for you?*

horn   Time to blow your own horn; horny; call somebody on the telephone; perhaps it is time to pull in your horns; a warning signal; someone horning in on your territory; a horn of plenty. *What dilemma has you on the horns of indecision?*

hornet Community living; being painfully stung; stirring up a hornet's nest. *Who are you mad at?*

horoscope   Looking to the stars for answers; check out your full horoscope, not just your sun sign; a birthday to remember. *What scope are you horrified of seeing?*

horror seeing too many late night horror shows; giving yourself a good scare. *What inner demons do you need to look at?*

horse   Powerful, instinctual urges; having trouble saying something; working too hard; a loyal friend; too much horsing around; someone showing you a horse of a different colour; being hoarse; good old fashioned horse sense is needed; being in control; feeling strong and free. *What are you putting your money on?*

horseshoe   Good luck. *Who is horsing around with you that you would like to shoo away?*

hose   **A** hoser; protect your legs; something needs a good hosing down. *Are you getting enough water to drink?*

hospice   Getting ready to reemerge back into nonphysical; care; a quiet goodbye. *What is your connection with hospice?*

hospital   Health concern; time for a check up; wanting to be cared for; memory of a hospital visit. *What do you need to feel better?*

host/hostess   Being responsible for the entertainment; looking after someone; being polite and ever-so-nice; a multitude; where a parasite lives. *When did you last give, or go to, a party?*

hostage   Having to do something you don't want to do; loss of freedom. *What or who is holding you hostage?*

hostel   A place of comfort; temporary lodgings; an unfriendly person. *Who are you feeling hostile toward?*

hot   Lots of ideas;   feeling under fire; getting hot under the collar; making it hot for someone; blowing hot and cold; someone full of hot air. *Who or what is too hot to handle?*

hot dog   Driving too fast; eating too fast; a dog with a fever. *Who eats lots of hot dogs?*

hotel   Temporary residence; traveling; needing to get away for a while; socializing. *When were you last in a hotel?*

hound   Woebegone; feeling like a dog; working like a dog; being treated like a dog. *Who or what is hounding you?*

hour   Now is the hour; experiencing the present; owning something with someone. *What important time has come up for you now?*

hourglass   An impossible figure; seeing through time; Barbie doll. *What do you do that takes an hour?*

house   Inner self; where you feel comfortable and cared for; a need to settle down; something you do could bring down the house; time to clean up; offering something on the house; time to clean up your act. (Dreaming about a house often represents various parts of yourself. See **attic**, **basement**, **kitchen**, etc.) *What part(s) of yourself have you been exploring lately? Or hiding?*

houseboat   Wanting to settle down, yet keep moving at the same time; just sailing along. *What part of you wants to float away?*

housecoat   Get out of the house; repainting a house. *What are you covering up?*

housekeeper   Feeling responsible for the whole house; looking after too many people; wanting to stay where you are. *Who says you can't keep your house?*

housework   Repetitious; never done; a house that is too much work; working on yourself; feeling nervous about working outside your home. *What are you avoiding by doing too much housework?*

howl   Someone in pain; worshiping the moon; needing attention. *Who has been howling at you and what for?*

hug   Wanting to be held and touched more; being uncomfortable with physical contact; feeling lonely; keeping close to shore. *Who can you hug today?*

huge Feeling small and insignificant; things beginning to feel too big for you; pay attention to what was huge in the dream. *What big thing is challenging you right now?*

hula A desire for a Hawaiian holiday; speaking with your hands and body; telling your story through gesture. *When did you last have a tropical holiday?*

hum   Not knowing what words to say; in tune; happy; a motor running; a hum of activity; ho-hum, how boring. *What is moving along smoothly for you right now?*

humiliate   Feeling ashamed; lowered self-respect. *What do you feel humiliated about and what can you do to regain your dignity?*

hummingbird   Incredibly swift; having the ability to eat on the fly or on the run. *What is moving so fast around you that you can hardly see it?*

hunger   Yearning for something you don't have; eating the wrong kinds of foods; feeling empty. *What are you craving?*

hunt   Searching for something; tracking; looking after your basic needs; feeling hunted. *What have you lost?*

hurdle Getting over obstacles; throwing yourself into your work; moving too quickly. *What hurdle are you faced with now?*

hurricane   Things beginning to whirl around you; feeling out of control; confusion; too much going on; a big wind bag around. *What thoughts are flying by that you are missing?*

hurt   In pain; a need to look after yourself; a warning. *What is hurting you so much?*

husband   A friend and companion; someone to look after; someone who gives comfort: an intimate relationship. *Who did the husband in the dream remind you of?*

hut   Simple living quarters; basic; a circle of men in tight pants. *Who lives in a hut?*

hydrant   Marking your territory; a place to cool off; give it some room; perhaps you need more water. *Where are you parked too close to something?*

hydro   Energy source; water power; electrical power; needing to drink more water. *Have you checked your water source lately?*

hyena   Being laughed at; laughing at another. *What is eating you?*

hymn   Songs of praise. *Which "him" are you concerned with?*

hypnotist   Under the spell of another; an altered state; a need to relax and let go; being afraid others will make a fool of you. *What do you feel you are being hypnotized by and have no control over?*

hypocrite   Acting so good but not really sincere; pretending. *Who is saying the opposite of what they really think?*

hypodermic   Something getting under your skin; needing an infusion of energy. *Who or what is needling you these days?*

hysterical   Losing control;   making a mountain out of a molehill. *What are you a little worried about?*

Within the self's inviolate nature
waits your prize in dreamed repose
for your minds to re-awaken
to the dawn that each heart knows

August 16, 2004

Ruth Cunningham

I

woken by thunder
and a dream of such beauty
flying within song
Nora Leonard

I   Self in the dream; notice the actions and thoughts of the I character in your dream and how this character is both like and unlike yourself in waking life; centre of the dream; eye. *How does the I in your dream reveal your true feelings?*

ice   A frozen, rigid, inaccessible person; cold, unfeeling; closing your heart to someone and to yourself; cautious beginnings as you break the ice in a new venture. *Who is the Ice Queen?*

iceberg   Part of you splintering off; don't be so hard on yourself; south or north pole; the larger part is under the surface. *Who would you describe as an iceberg?*

icebox   Keeping cool; preserving something; something that is unchangeable. *What skills and talents have you put on ice?*

ice cream   Children indicated; luxury and enjoyment; carefree; taking a holiday from the daily grind; relationship with mother may be cold. *What is too cold to be skimmed off?*

ice skates   Skating on thin ice; gliding over the surface of things; a way to enjoy winter. *When did you last go ice-skating?*

icicle   Sharp, cold; cutting remarks; feeling defensive and on guard. *Who is tall, lean and cold-hearted?*

icing   Sweet remarks on top; covering up mistakes; sugary and insincere. *What are you covering up with fancy words?*

identification A shift in self-image and/or self-presentation; a fear of losing identity. *How is your identity changing?*

idiot   Feeling inferior, or superior; performance anxiety; unable to meet expectations at work. *How are you putting yourself down?*

idol   Lazy, idle; looking up to someone; high dreams, a chance at fame. *Who have you been putting on a pedestal?*

igloo   Cold home environment; feeling enclosed; no freedom or privacy. *Who lives in a cold house?*

ignition   Getting things started; having the spark to do it; starting the fire of ideas. *What new venture are you excited about?*

illness   Possible health issue; resisting who you really are; feeling weak and in need of rest; having too high expectations of yourself. *Who is making themselves sick?*

illegal   Not following the proper channels; looking into legal matters; moral dilemma. *What are you considering that your inner-self disapproves of?*

illegitimate   Not following the laws or rules; fear of what people will say; unsure of your birthright. *What needs to be joined before you can give birth to something?*

illiterate   Unable to read between the lines; inability to write your own thoughts; feeling inferior. *Who are you not reading correctly?*

illuminate   Shining forth; hiding your light under a bushel; a clear explanation needed. *What, or who, has been in the dark too long?*

illustration   A need for clarification; demonstrate what you mean; give examples. *What is your dream drawing to your attention?*

image   Looking at yourself through different eyes; comparing your real image with your virtual image. *What is out of sync about your self-image?*

imitation   Copying; not following through on your own ideas and intuitions; accepting poor substitutes for what you really want; accepting dependency as a substitute for true love. *Where have you accepted an inferior substitute for what you really want?*

immense   Something huge in your dream that you have been minimizing in waking life; something is much larger than you want to believe. *How are you making light of a profound situation?*

immerse Get involved; dive in; getting in too deep. *Who is overly immersed in something, to the neglect of something else?*

immigrate   Gathering information from other sources; from another country. *What part of yourself have you left behind?*

immobile   Unable to move freely; unable to make a decision and act on it; someone telling you what to do; boss unwilling to delegate responsibilities; feeling trapped. *What is frustrating you?*

immortal   Fear of death; assurance from the unconscious that we do live forever; strong spiritual symbol; a connection with your inner self. *What spiritual message is the dream immortal bringing?*

immovable Stuck; refusing to change; unable to move forward; scared; insecure. *Who is being stubborn?*

imp A little rascal; a trickster; someone playing a joke; see the funny side. *Where could you act more spontaneously?*

impale Feeling like a target; victimized; caught in a trap; unfairly accused of wrong doing; sexuality. *Who has stabbed you in public?*

impatient Feeling frustrated; going along at someone else's slower pace; smothering or dampening your natural enthusiasm. *What are you worried about not getting done in time and what is the hurry?*

impersonate Someone pretending to be who they are not; lack of confidence; let go of the act. *Who would you like to be?*

impolite Being overly polite; going out of your way to say nice things but thinking the opposite; conforming to social norms. *Where would you like to practice some honest feedback for a change?*

import Taking something in; news from another country; paying attention. (see **immigrate**) *What do you need from someone?*

impossible An overly optimistic attitude about what can be achieved; feeling blocked; unable to move through a barrier. *Who is dreaming the impossible dream?*

impotent A loss of power, feeling less than, frustration. *What will happen if you stand up and say what you think?*

incense Meditation; using one's sense of smell to relax; spiritual symbol; getting in touch with yourself; ritualizing a transition in your life; raging. *Who is being rude to you?*

incest   Inappropriate sexual behaviour; protection needed; mixed up love feelings, violation. *Who, or what, is being inappropriate?*

incinerator   Wanting to make a dramatic change; intending to get rid of a bad habit or attitude; burning old memories; wishing to forget the past. *What would you like to trash and burn?*

inch   Slow moving, step by step; near to something; impatient. *What are you inches from achieving?*

incline   Working your way back to the top; struggling and striving to get ahead; using all your energy to move forward; working hard. *What do you have an inclination to do?*

income tax   Keeping track of your money; feeling over taxed; frustration; feeling responsible for others. *What activity is presently overtaxing you?*

incomplete   Not getting a project done on time; having a new demand before something else has been finished; wishing for closure on an old relationship. *What finishing touch have you overlooked?*

incubator   Keeping things safe while they develop more strength; looking after premature ideas; keeping an even temperature. *What new plans are you hatching?*

index   Keeping track of things; inability to find things; looking for something. *Where is your dream pointing?*

Indian   A natural or wild person; freedom; nonconforming; spirituality tied to the Earth; placing significance on dreaming and visioning; strong sense of community; India. (see **native**) *How can you benefit from the wisdom of aboriginal people?*

indigestion   Not eating properly; not paying close enough attention to your diet; poor combination of foods; food allergy may be indicated; a problem processing emotions.   *What is turning your stomach?*

indoors Spending too much time inside; not getting enough exercise; too much time away from your social group.   *Who is being defended from outside influences?*

infidelity   Worries about a partner being unfaithful; trouble committing. *Who is feeling guilty about being attracted to another?*

inheritance   Money or prize coming to you; attributes inherited from your parents and grandparents; and identity too dependent on how one resemble a parent.   *Who is banking on an inheritance?*

initiation   Going through a trial in order to be accepted; a new challenge; seeking approval from an admired person or group.   *What are you being initiated into, and what will this prove about you?*

injection   Being given something forcibly; throwing in your two-cents worth. *What do you need to receive?*

injure Moving too quickly; not watching what you are doing; becoming careless; not taking safety precautions; pushing yourself too hard.   *Where is the injury on your body in the dream and how might it alert you to a waking life risk?*

ink   writing letters by hand instead of the computer; making something official. *What is hiding under that protective cover?*

inn Going into new places; taking a holiday in the British Isles; looking inward. *What is in you that you are not expressing?*

insane A crazy idea; incompetent; way out, wild thoughts. *What are you contemplating that others would consider crazy?*

insect Someone/something repulsive; something small and scary; someone you despise and could easily overwhelm; things creeping along too slowly for you; the ability to hang in. *What's bugging you?*

inside Following the beaten track; approval-seeking; trying hard to please everyone. *What can you set free?*

insignia Being part of the club; conformity; mark of identity; family history or organization; feeling important because of job or position. *What signifies you as being who you are?*

insole Knowing you are a soul; needing help in walking through life; a soft cushion. *What in your soul needs expression?*

inspect Looking intently: under a microscope; checking things out first. *What do you need to look over?*

inspector Monitoring the action; inner authority figure; male – inspector father figure; female mother figure. *Who is in charge?*

institution Solid; treated like a number; too many rules to follow; being part of something larger than yourself; seeming to last forever; parents; security. *What institution supports you or limits you?*

instrument Playing music; feeling used; having the correct tool for the job; playing an important part. *Who can be instrumental in helping you?*

insulation Protection from the cold; feeling separated from others; apart. *From what, or who, are you insulating yourself?*

insurance   Feeling nervous; at risk; being careless; something you value should be insured; having a back up plan; insurance payment past due. *Who needs assurance?*

intermission   Taking a break; time to socialize; an inside mission. *How could you take a break from your daily grind?*

interrogate   Feeling under pressure to confess; getting or giving sensitive information. *What are you holding back?*

interrupt   Being stopped or slowed down; losing the flow; losing your train of thought and where you are going; being distracted. *How are you stopping yourself from getting on with it?*

intersection   Two major forces meeting; x marks the spot; confrontation and change. *What is intersecting what?*

interview Applying for a job; performance anxiety; wanting a change of profession. *Who could you practice with beforehand?*

invalid   Unable to perform; knowing someone who is challenged physically, or psychologically; being discounted and overlooked; loss of credibility. *What are you invalidating in yourself?*

invention   New ideas; thinking up a new way to do something; reinventing yourself. *How are you recreating yourself today?*

inventory Taking stock; counting up what you have and what you need. *What special things do you value about yourself?*

invisible   Feeling unimportant; unnoticed, or not taken seriously; not paying attention to something important right in front of you. *Who is too good at blending in?*

invitation Wanting to be included; feeling left out, and rejected; message to get in touch with a person who's doing the inviting in your dream. *Who would you like to invite to join you?*

invoice Something owed; keeping track of what you have produced and what is out there; in good voice. *What needs to be voiced?*

iodine When healing hurts; eating kelp and seafood; something needs to be cleaned up. *What can heal your wound?*

iris The color of someone's eyes, Iris; the windows of the soul; romantic, mysterious; symbol of wholeness, as in circle and cycle. *Whose eyes have you been staring into?*

iron Strong, unbending, rigid; stubborn; too many irons in the fire; a gun; take quick action; feeling shackled; smoothing things out; things pressing in on you. *Who has a will of iron?*

island Being alone, self-sufficient, independent; believing you don't need anyone else; isolation; holiday; you have landed. *Who lives on an island or is visiting one?*

itch Annoying insects around; allergy alert; attention getter; a desire to move; restlessness. *What are you itching to do?*
ivory Piano-player; playing dice; withdrawal into an ivory tower. *Who or what is precious and worth protecting?*

ivy Something getting the better of you; quick growth; feeling surrounded; physical changes; old buildings indicated; an ivy league school; a person named Ivy. *Who is the snob?*

Hiding in life's folds and creases
facts and fiction — lies and truths
shake them out — their fit is perfect
joy to wear their living hues

Jan. 29, 1987
                    Ruth Cunningham

when I was a child
a dream snake licked my tongue, ears
such deep dark knowing
Nora Leonard

J

jack   Help in supporting something heavy; Jack; playing childish games; feeling inferior. *Who is nimble and quick?*

jackal   Working like a dog; not appreciated; doing menial tasks; feeling like an unsung hero; having little glory. *How are you underestimating your contribution?*

jacket   Feeling vulnerable and exposed; needing to protect yourself from nosey people; a coverup. *What's under the jacket?*

jack-in-the-box   Be careful; a person named Jack who keeps jumping out at you. *What surprising thing has popped up recently?*

jack-o-lantern Autumn; harvesting what you sowed in the spring; childhood memories. *If the jack-o-lantern in your dream could speak to you, what would it say?*

jackpot   Good luck coming your way; waiting for that big win; Jack on the pot. *Who is about to hit the jackpot?*

jade   Worn-out; cynical and tired; someone who has a jade plant or wears jade. *How are you being naive?*

jaguar   A beautiful and expensive car; prowess in the workplace with rich rewards; *Who is as crafty as a cat?*

jail   Fear of commitment or getting caught; having too many inner demands and expectations; a run   in with authority; recrimination; consequences of dishonesty; self-punishment. *How can you break out of that inner prison you've constructed for yourself?*

jam   Stuck; a situation that appears very sweet, but is really quite sticky and uncomfortable; caught between two opposing forces and having to choose a side, a sweet situation. *Who's in a jam?*

janitor   Unappreciated by others; having to clean up other peoples' messes. *Where are you expected to clean up others' mistakes?*

jar   Containing your emotions; feeling watched and judged; self conscious; half-opened; something shaking your composure; a quarrel. *Who is living in a glass house?*

jaw   All talk, no action; feeling victimized and tense; sticking your jaw out. *Who is doing all the gabbing?*

jay   Freedom of movement; beautiful king of the hill; making an awful racket; paying attention when you cross the street. *Whose name begins with the letter J?*

jazz   New Orleans; creative, unusual and exotic ideas; free and unconstrained. *Who is jazzing you?*

jealous   Thinking you can't have it too; a belief in scarcity; feeling unloved and unappreciated; not recognizing your own positive traits. *In what areas of your life do you feel insecure?*

jeans   Family ties and inheritance; strong and ready for work, but stylish too; unpretentious; looking young and rugged. *Who do you know who wears jeans most of the time?*

jeep   Carefree and young; able to traverse unpredictable territory; going off on your own; connection with the military.   *Where are you venturing off on your own?*

jelly   Sweet delicious food; too wishy-washy; feeling nervous, unsteady; someone has tremendous influence and power over you. *When do your legs turn to jelly?*

jellyfish   Harmless looking but deadly; just floating along; *Danger in the deep. Who is unapproachable?*

jester someone who makes jokes to cover up their nervousness and embarrassment; having to perform and be entertaining when one wrong joke could land you in serious trouble. *Who is being the joker?*

Jesus   Love, kindness, gentleness, forgiveness, healing, eternal life; a vision from the inner self carrying a message that you are on the right track spiritually; your inner self is present and in tune with what you want. (See **Christ**)   *What special message did this dream-figure of Jesus convey that can enrich you and bring peace of mind?*

jet   flying high; excitement and travel are indicated; getting swept off your feet; remembering to keep your feet firmly planted on the ground as you move to grab this opportunity.   *Who is taking a trip?*

jewel   Symbol of the inner self; acquiring riches may be your desire; being reminded that it is your inner wealth that counts.   *What part of yourself do you value most?*

jig   Dancing as fast as you can to keep up with the flow; fancy-stepping to perform for someone; casting your line.   *What can you do that would make your job easier?*

jigsaw   Puzzled; a missing piece; too many pieces; not enough information to know how it will all fit together; cutting out an irregular pattern. *What part of your life is a puzzle and how is your dream pointing to the missing piece?*

job   Concerns about a job; performance worries;   problems with co-workers; fear of losing a job. *Whose job is it?*

jockey   In touch with your instincts; listen to your body and what it is guiding you to do; moving very fast; someone who wears jockey shorts. *Where are you jockeying for position?*

jog   Moving along at an even pace; steadiness; self- sufficient and goal orientated; remembering something; exercising.   *What do you think about when you're jogging?*

joke   Taking life too seriously; making light of a serious issue; remembering to see the humour in life. *Who is just a joke?*

journal   A reminder to keep up your dream journal; looking back in your journal for clues. *What has journal-keeping taught you?*

journey   Spiritual seeking; the journey is the goal; taking a trip. *What journey are you presently on?*

joyful   Connection to your inner self; affirmation. *How is your dream showing you things to feel joyful about?*

judge   Feeling criticized and measured; facing the consequences; feeling intimidated by someone in power. *Who is judging you?*

jug   A heavy container; someone in jail; getting a handle on something. *Who's doing a large part of the chores?*

juggle   Too much to do; being confused and stressed; feeling caught between opposing views; having money difficulties and challenges. *Who, or what, are you juggling?*

juice   Feeling excited; drink plenty of juice; squeezing the goodness out of life; check your batteries. *What juicy bit of news have you heard lately?*

jump   Feeling jittery; too many responsibilities; avoiding getting caught; one step ahead; eager to get something done. *Who is asking how high, when ordered to jump?*

jungle   Wanting to escape; inner growth; caught in a mess; protecting the endangered. *Who wants to be wild and free?*

junk   Time to get organized; wanting change; being hard on yourself; snagged by perfectionism; someone involved with drugs; Chinese boat. *What would you like to junk?*

jury   Feeling guilty; fear of getting caught; telling lies to oneself; being phoney. *Who do you feel judged by?*

"Our dreams reveal the distinction
between real and unreal to be a fiction."
Anonymous

Silence buzzing — magic secrets
language that the heart recalls
those who listen still can hear us
echo through their own mind's halls

Jan. 11, 1987
                    Ruth Cunningham

K

my psyche in a swamp
I dream of Mayan icons;
tangled growth of soul
Nora Leonard

kaleidoscope   Confusion; too much   information at once; pieces beginning to fall together; missing some important information; visual patterns; random beauty. *What are you seeing with one eye?*

kangaroo   Australia; protective   mother; working hard for children and others who depend on you; determination and strength; protecting your pouch; someone illegally holding court.   *How are you keeping your children in your pocket?*

karate   Self-protection; not needing weapons; fast on your feet; physically fit. *Who are you fighting with your bare hands?*

kayak   Travelling alone; protected as you move; if you turn over you will automatically right yourself; a sport's lover.   *Are you paddling upstream or downstream?*

kazoo   **M**aking childish music; some annoying sound; just humming your way through life. *Where were you when you last heard a kazoo and what is similar about this for you now?*

keelhaul   Being roughly treated; inhumane punishment; feelings as if you been through the wringer; getting dunked. *Who has been severely rebuked?*

keepsake   Special memories; feelings and thoughts related to aging. *What is important to keep and for whose sake?*

keg   Eating out; drinking; good times may be distracting you; storing something. *Who or what is about to explode?*

kelp   Reminder to eat seaweed; ocean; deep unconscious, growing hopefulness, new possibilities and positive change. *What significance is the east coast to you?*

kennel   Looking after a dog; listening to your natural inclinations; Protection. *Who is in the dog house?*

kerchief Hiding your thoughts; afraid of thoughts: feeling defensive and self conscious; needing protection from the outside world. *Who is hiding their ambition behind feminine wiles?*

ketchup   Behind in something and trying to catch up; covering up the flavour of life, hamburgers/ hotdogs. *Who is faking being hurt?*

kettle Feeling pressured, boiling over; needing to blow off steam; in a fix; time to relax and think things over before taking any action. *Who is steaming mad?*

key   You have all the tools you need to unlock the truth; finding the central piece of the issue; gaining access to the complete solution; hitting the right key; being well prepared; anxious about something. *Who is the key player in this life dilemma?*

keyboard   A writer; musician; spending too much time at the computer. *Who do you know who plays a keyboard?*

kick   A kick in the pants; feeling abused; a kickback; lying around doing nothing; a big start off; time to kick up your heels; getting a kick out of life. *Why do you want to kick yourself?*

kid   Childhood memories; concern about a child; treating someone with kid gloves; kidding around. *How are you neglecting to listen to the kid in you?*

kidnap   Held hostage; someone taking the credit for work you have done; making sure your kids are getting enough rest.   *What are you stealing away from yourself?*

kidney Health issue related to urination; suppressed anger; eating too much organ meat. *Who are you pissed off with?*

kill   Angry at someone for what you hate in yourself; cutting off a supply or your energy; aggression; dressed to kill. (see **murder**) *What part of yourself have you been killing off?*

kiln   Creating things with heat; someone is getting all fired up. Packed in a hot situation. *Who is the potter you know?*

kilt   Scotland; family traditions; freedom from oppression and rebellion; pride of country; keeping the secret of what's under the kilt; belonging to a clan; identification. *Who wears a kilt?*

kimono Time to relax; covering up your sleeping identity; Japanese association. *Who's lives in their housecoat?*

kindergarten   Starting over again; returning to the basics; early school feelings surfacing; inexperienced and scared. *Who needs to remember an earlier time?*

king   Male authority figure; having power and financial security; the head, the leader; father; boss. *Whose approval do you seek that reminds you of dear old dad?*

kiosk   Feeling cramped; not enough space; a shelter. *What are you trying to sell yourself on?*

kiss   A call to wake up; sexuality; wanting to connect with another; kiss and tell;   kissing cousin; a kiss of death/ kiss of life.   *Who's waiting for Prince or Princess Charming to come into their life?*

kit   Small and vulnerable; getting the right equipment. *What pieces can you put together to make one neat package?*

kitchen   Transformation; mother's role; nurturing, food and warmth; putting yummy things together; nice smells; feeling satisfied. *Who can you turn to for support?*

kite   Leisure and childlike joy; needing to relax; wanting an from adult responsibilities; suppressed anger; holding tight at your end. *Who would you like to tell to go fly a kite?*

kitten   A young and quickly developing part of yourself;   needing care and support; vulnerability and nervousness; holding high stakes (kitty). *Who is as playful as a kitten?*

knapsack   Desire to travel light; carrying your life around on your back; stuffing it all back there; behind you; time to take a nap, school. *What is in your knapsack and where do you want to go?*

knee   A quick response; prayer and meditation; feeling beaten and put down; knee-deep into something; someone knee-high. *What is bringing you to your knees?*

knife   A tool or a weapon; cutting away the excess; getting stabbed in the heart; a cutting remark; an operation; someone with a strong accent. *What, or who, do you need to cut out of your life?*

knight   Bravery; blind dedication to a cause; wanting someone to come and rescue you; old fashioned way of settling a score, a damsel in distress. (see **night***) Who acts like a knight in shining armour?*

knit   Bringing things together; staying warm; frowning; following a pattern; a nit picker. *Who is the knitter?*

knob   An opportunity; open the door with an open mind; someone trying to communicate with you; English slang.   *What are you grasping for?*

knock   Opportunity waiting; feeling pushed around; knocking your head against a hard wall; knocking something into shape; school of hard knocks. *Who is not responding to the constant knocking?*

knot   Feelings of tension and stress; feeling frustrated and unable to move forward; needing to release pressure in your back and stomach; saying no too often. *Whose jammies are in a knot?*

knuckle   Time to get down to some hard work; feeling you want to punch someone; sore knuckles (see **fingers**).   *Where do you feel you are under someone else's power?*

koan   Logical reasoning sometimes is not enough. *What is the riddle you need to solve?*

kosher   Doing it correctly; following the rules; eating out with Jewish friends; some things that have to be kept separate.   *Who is feeling restricted by custom or laws?*

Filling up the heart's deep river
swifter roars the flow of time
on its foaming crest there quivers
every dreamer's dream divine

Jan. 12, 1987
Ruth Cunningham

*funny how a dream
could feel so much more real
than my reality
Linda Mazuranic*

L

laboratory Time to experiment with new ways to approach problems; mixing elements of your life together in new and innovative ways. *Which of your old problem solving approaches are not working as well as they used to?*

labyrinth Getting lost; things becoming too confusing; many twists and turns. *Which inner beast haven't you faced?*

lace Old fashioned dress; feminine; striking out at someone; something needs spiking up; grandmother. *What uncomfortable situation are you being squeezed into?*

ladder Climbing the social or professional ladder; working your way to the top; the spine may also be indicated; kundalini energy. *What is the ladder taking you to, or away from, in the dream?*

lady-bug Good-luck; a child's favourite bug; time to fly away home. *Who is all fired up about their new project?*

lake Feeling overwhelmed by strong emotions; plunging into spiritual seeking; thirsty; fresh water. *Which lake is significant?*

lamb Leaping and cavorting; gentleness, quiet, and vulnerability meek and mild; sacrifice. *Where are you most vulnerable?*

lamp   Highlighting an issue; fear of darkness; loneliness; burning the midnight oil. *Who can shed some light on your problem?*

land   Coming down to earth; a need to be grounded; someone with their head in the clouds; consequences of actions; time for completion. *Who is feeling frantic and scattered?*

landing   Arriving; having feet firmly planted; rooted to the ground. *What has landed in your lap lately?*

landscape   Designing your place; cleaning up your own backyard; impressing your neighbours. *How long has it been since you have weeded out negative self criticism?*

lane   On a narrow path; going the back way; staying in your own lane; change lanes carefully. *Who is driving in the fast lane?*

lap   Aa need for comfort and nurturing; stress-reduction indicated; doing too many laps; tired out;   look at what is over lapping and causing problems; eagerly taking it all in; something that has fallen into your lap. *Who can offer you comfort and protection?*

lard   Fats in the diet; needing ease of entry; hot and greasy, getting burned, a fat person. *Who is about to jump out of the frying pan and into the fire?*

laser   Accuracy, precision and focus; shedding light; moving with precision; a printer. *Where do you need to narrow your focus?*

last   Being last; final; afterthought; the end of something; hanging in against all odds; having enough; good-fitting shoes. *Who is being the nice guy?*

late   Lack of preparation and planning; not wanting to do something; dragging your feet. *Who is always late?*

latex   Protection from germs and hot water; being flexible and following someone else's direction. *Who is diving into potentially painful situations without protection?*

laugh   Needing a vacation; going to a play; taking up a hobby; reminding you of a funny time; something you can just laugh off; having the last laugh; laughing up your sleeve; laughing on the other side of your mouth. *Who is being too serious?*

laundry   Cleaning; personality change; letting shameful secrets out; weekly chores; illegal activities. *Who are you looking after?*

law   Abiding by the rules; a rebellious spirit; going strictly by the book; a lawyer. *Who is laying down the law?*

lawn   Caring for things for appearance's sake; tending to your own backyard; condition of dream lawn reflects your inner emotional condition. *Who is not minding their business and is only concerned with what other people think?*

lay   A need to rest; put down your load; someone laying heavy emotion on you; setting your course; putting something aside; lying in wait; feeling exposed; taking a break in your journey; heading directly into the wind and then stand still; from the ordinary people; not professional; lay lines. *Who is laying down on the job?*

lazy   Not living up to your potential; lack of confidence in one's ability; time to rest. *How are you expecting too much of yourself?*

lead   Leadership; slowness or hesitancy about taking the lead; shyness and worry about failing; showing the way to others; being ahead of others; making the first play. *Who is being asked to take the lead, but doesn't really want the responsibility?*

leaf   Time for a change in attitude; changing your colours; letting go; veins; following someone's example; someone who reads a lot. (see **leave***) What new leaf has turned up for you?*

leak   A drain on your energy; someone telling secrets; having to urinate while dreaming. *Where are you allowing your thoughts to leak out instead of deliberately directing them?*

leap   Risk taking; moving in leaps and bounds; taking a leap in the dark or a leap into the unknown.. *What is stopping you from taking the leap?*

leather   Needing a protective covering; animal instincts; motorcyclists. *Who's been out in the sun too long?*

leave   Saying goodbye; the end of something; time to move on; stop doing something; giving yourself permission to go off duty. *What did you leave out?*

lecture   Time for information gathering; attending a lecture; lecturing and not listening; a bossy person; telling someone off. *Who does the lecturer remind you of?*

ledge   On the edge; risky business where one wrong move means you could take a tumble. *Where are you on the edge?*

left An awkward move; creativity; something previously unconscious coming to awareness; leaving something behind; liberal thinking; left-brained;   rational, sequential thinking; left handed.   *Who, or what, have you left?*

leg   Standing up for yourself; on the last leg of a journey; having a leg to stand on; on your last legs; tired; pulling someone's leg; time to hurry up and shake a leg. *How are you trying to get a leg up?*

lemon   A sour taste; making lemonade; a bad deal; Jack Lemon, invisible writing. *What has gone sour?*

lens   Focusing in on the details; a photographer; making things clearer; something that Len owns; be sure you are looking through the correct end. *What do you need to look at more closely?*

leopard   Trust your instincts; a large cat; camouflage;, being truthful about who you really are. *Who thinks they can't change?*

lesbian   Loving women; a woman you would really like to get close to; a woman with whom you share much in common; loving your own femininity, a courageous woman. *Who is the woman who has qualities you would like to develop in yourself?*

letter   Communication from someone you haven't seen for a long time; it may be time to let her do it; being exact and keeping to the letter. *Who would you like to send a letter to?*

lettuce   Permission to the group; eating greens; wilting. *Who is getting limp?*

lever   Setting a new project into motion; getting help; working hard. Where some leverage help?

liar   Telling or hearing a lie; lying around; hiding the truth. *Who are you trying to fool?*

library Finding information; homework; getting organized; a lover of books; having your nose in a book; lots of books. *Where can you go to get the information you need?*

license Needing permission; getting the right papers; car/dog/fishing license; agent 007. *Who is in danger of losing their license?*

lick Receiving punishment; healing wounds; making something presentable by licking it into shape; someone not doing their share or lick of work; giving something a lick and a promise; acknowledgment; sexuality. *Who is ready for a lolly pop?*

lid Putting a stop to explosive emotional reactions; top of something; keeping secrets; not allowing the truth to come out; someone ready to flip their lid; keep your hat on. *Where is the pressure building up?*

lie A deceit; hiding something; fear of being found out; lying down on the job. *Who is not being truthful with you?*

life buoy Something to hold on to when you are in danger of drowning or sinking; a warning that you are getting close to the rocks. *Who's the boy in your life?*

life guard Someone looking out for you; therapist or healer; a strong muscular man or woman. *Who needs guarding or saving?*

lift Feeling down; needing to be cheered up; displaying something on high; someone stealing; a way to get to the top of the hill, an elevator, needing help to stand tall. *Who is getting a free ride?*

light Support; new knowledge; illumination; viewing things in the right light; bringing something to light; a light burden; making light of it; finding the answer; meditation; spirituality. *What needs more light?*

lighthouse   A beacon; holding the light; help is on the way; moving to a house with more space and light; paying attention to the signal. *What are you getting dangerously close to?*

lightning   Strong feelings; flashes of anger and frustration; sudden insight. *What needs to hit you like a bolt of lightning for you to get it?*

lilac New growth; spring in the air; romance, beauty, and appreciation of nature; June. *Where do you normally go to revive yourself?*

lily   Erotic feelings; sexuality can be   indicated; association with Quebec or France; Easter; pure; delicate.   *Who is in the mood for a little romance?*

limp   Trouble moving forward; not centered; moving slowly; soft and flabby; performance anxiety. *What is out of balance?*

line   Having things in order; knowing what to say; dropping someone a short note; something to do with your family line; bring something into line or into agreement; can't decide for one side or the other; a protective layer; money in your pockets; waiting in line; following a narrow line. *What is written between the lines?*

lining   Something beautiful beneath the surface; not obvious to the naked eye. *What is really going on underneath it all?*

link   Tying things together; the bond that joins people; thing or position; playing golf. *What is the bond between you and another?*

lion   A powerful connection to your inner self; instincts; king; someone telling you lies;   a person born under the sign of Leo; self confident;   defying someone in their own space; a connection with Britain; getting your share; brave. *What are you pursuing?*

lioness   Female power; strong mother; moody and unpredictable; potentially lethal; pride. *Who is being fiercely protective?*

lip   Speaking out of turn; speaking ill of someone; wanting to kiss someone; sensuality; expressing   warm feelings toward someone; wanting to speak endearing words; being extra brave or firm;   paying lip service to something. *Who has been saying things off the top of their head?*

lipstick Sticking to what you say; insincerity; a sticky kiss. *What truth are you afraid to speak?*

liquid   Flowing freely; easily turned into cash; clear and bright; inner truth. *What new thoughts and feelings are pouring forth now?*

liquor   High spirits; changing your mental state; partying. *Who   do you know who drinks too much?*

list Too much to do and not enough time; organize your time and plan your work; something off balance and tipping to one side. *Who is attempting to do too many things at once?*

lizard   Moving quietly without anybody noticing; look at what you're dragon. *Who has slithered into your life?*

lobby   Fighting for a cause; a   public announcement; coming into something; throwing something away; going to the theatre. *What new adventure are you entering?*

lobster   Your natural home is the unconscious; someone with big claws; connection with east coast; at risk of sunburn. *Where do you feel as if you are being boiled alive?*

lock   Shutting yourself off emotionally; needing to raise or lower something to get through; time to adjust the level; let go of something lock, stock and barrel; someone you know with curly hair. *What has been locked away inside you for too long?*

locker   Putting something away for safe keeping; the right combination gets you in. *What part of you have you locked away?*

locket A small gift and favour from a loved one; lock it up. *Who from your past is playing an important role in your life now?*

log   Playing on the Internet a lot; keeping track of your journey; trees; getting in a log jam; constipation; not getting enough sleep. *What's as easy as falling off a log?*

lollipop   Childhood memories; sucking up to someone. *Who is trying to appease you with sweet talk?*

loom   Something appears large and indistinct; weaving the strands together; a weaver, intricate pattern. *What is threatening you?*

loop   A repeating pattern; right back where you started; what goes around comes around; a loop hole. *What loop are you caught up in?*

lost Finding something; feeling ungrounded and unsure; being lost in thought, TV show. *Where are you having trouble letting go?*

love Strong positive feeling; reconnecting with someone you love; the energy of the universe. *How can you express this spiritual feeling in your waking life?*

lover   Romance and sexual feelings indicated; a bonding between two different sides of yourself. *How does your dream lover's description sound like a part of you?*

luck Counting on something that's unreliable; believing that you have no control; someone feeling down on their luck; feeling confident. *What always turns out right for you?*

luggage Packing your feelings away; taking a trip; carrying extra baggage around. *What are you dragging behind you?*

lunatic Losing control; stiff repression; resolute, inflexible; a full moon. *Who is acting crazy around you?*

lunch Eating lightly; meeting with friends for lunch. *Who is "out to lunch"?*

lung Take a deep breath; something too close; confined; holding your breath; smoking too much. *What, or who, is suffocating you?*

"There are dreams and dreams,
and we must get rid of the assumption
that they all resemble each other."

Mary Arnold-Forster

M

how do dream gardens
deep-seated in such parched soul
keep on greening
Nora Leonard

machine   Being on automatic; mechanical help; a machine worker. *How can you change your life so that you have more choice?*

machinery   Feeling unappreciated and used; treated like a robot. *Where are you feeling like just another cog in the wheel?*

mad   Upset and angry; someone mad as a hatter; a foolish action. *What are you trying to do like mad?*

madness   Over stressed; worried; frightened. *When do you pretend to be calm, cool and collected but really don't feel that way inside?*

Madonna   Exhibitionism; sensual; a big star; mother image; divine mother. *When have you been toning down your natural exuberance and sensuality?*

Mafia   Feeling threatened; keeping secrets; family strength; feeling trapped. *What are you afraid of?*

magazine   Stories; easy reading; storing up explosive material. *What are you reading that is helpful to you now?*

magic   Fascination with the unexplained; amazing power; someone with fast hands. *How can you bring back the magic in your life?*

magician   A person with amazing abilities; things seem to come so easily to them; connected to your inner power. *Who do you admire for their ability to manifest and how can they be of help to you?*

magnet Attracted and repelled at the same time; being drawn to someone or something; attractive personality; stuck on something or someone. *What positive things do you want to attract to you?*

magnify   Focusing in on an issue; making something seem larger than it is. *What is your dream, or life, magnifying?*

mail   Receiving or sending an important message; a male in your life; a protective covering. *Who do you need to connect with that can help you?*

major An important issue; striking the right chord; a course of study; someone in the major leagues. *Who gives the orders?*

makeup   A lie or exaggeration; covering up your natural beauty; feeling insecure about yourself. *Who is making something up?*

mall   Showing you something in public; an addiction to shopping; *Who do you know who hangs out in malls?*

man   The masculine part of yourself;   acting in agreement as one man; being your own man; a man about town. *Who does the man in your dream remind you of?*

manager   Related to work; looking after things; an organizer; something beyond your control. *What needs to be managed better?*

mandala An important dream symbol; can indicate Self or soul, the eternal/spiritual part of you;   going into the centre; drawing it will enhance the experience. *What special gift does the mandala represent?*

manhole A whole man; be careful where you walk, a loud or big-mouthed man. *What man has left a hole in your life?*

manicure Trying to cure or fix a man; keeping your claws sharp. *What special occasion is coming up?*

mannequin Someone being treated like a dummy; overly concerned with clothes; a small man. *Who's the clothes horse?*

manuscript The plot and story of your life; start keeping a diary along with your dream journal; a story that needs to be told. *What is the main plot of your story?*

map Needing directions: seeking a treasure; something off the map; something worthwhile about to be put on the map. *How is your dream map guiding you?*

maple Connection with Canada; sweet and syrupy; hockey team; loyalty. *What sap is running after you?*

marathon Feeling exhausted; thinking it will never end; a long run. *What do you wish you'd never started?*

marble Hard; childhood games; a crazy person. *Who do you know who is cold, beautiful and hard to reach?*

march Keeping in step; going along with others; peer pressure to conform; March; something is moving forward; as mad as a March hare. *Are you marching to your own drummer? If not, why not?*

marijuana Altered state of consciousness; a need to escape; spending too much time in reflection and not enough time acting. *How else could you reach that good feeling place?*

marionette   Being all tied up; feeling as if someone is pulling your strings; putting on an act. *Where do you feel out of control?*

market Selling your skills and talents; looking for a different place or type of employment; speculating on the stock exchange; reconsider the market value; fresh produce.   *What does your dream have to say about employment?*

marquee   Wanting approval; needing to see your name in lights; smitten with fame; making a fancy entrance.   *What announcement about yourself do you want on the marquee?*

marriage A uniting of different aspects of yourself; romance; acceptance and tolerance; a happy couple. *Who is your ideal mate?*

martyr   Giving your all and not being appreciated; a strong belief or faith; pretending to suffer to get attention.   *Who is the long suffering person?*

mask Covering up the truth; hiding your true self from others; someone putting on a false face. *How have you been keeping your true self hidden from a loved one?*

massage   Needing to relax; working too many hours and not taking time to enjoy yourself; enjoying sensuality to relieve tension; get your blood circulating. *How does your dream show you a way to improve the quality of your life?*

masturbate   Pleasing yourself; looking after your own needs; not having your sexual needs met; feeling guilty or ashamed. *What nice thing can you do for yourself today?*

mat   The need for padding; protection underneath; something tangled together; framing an image; dull; Mat or Matthew. *What can you do to make your life shinier?*

match   Lighting a fire; something equal; a game or contest; a perfect pair. *What would be the right match for you?*

math   Something not adding up; divide and conquer; a situation multiplying; take a good measure; get the right quantity. *What do you need to subtract from your life?*

mattress   Making love; dreaming; needing more sleep; soft and cozy; relaxing. *What are you hiding in your mattress?*

maze   Confusion; not knowing which direction to take next; inability to act and move forward; something corny. *Where are you lost and confused and how is your dream pointing a way out?*

meadow   Serenity; nature; many flowers; appreciating the country. *When have you last frolicked in a meadow?*

meal   Hungry for affection; nurturance; lacking in sustenance; being treated as a meal ticket. *How can you feed yourself better?*

meat   Angry; biting off more than you can chew; taking a bite out of someone; the real issue. *What important meeting is coming up?*

mechanical Automatic and without expression; have your car or some other machine checked out; learning the mechanics of something. *What part of your life have you put on automatic pilot?*

medal   wanting recognition; someone interfering with others' affairs (see **metal**). *What do you deserve a medal for?*

medicine   Healing; looking for a cure; taking something unpleasant; sacred or special ceremonies; magical powers.   *How can you better take care of yourself?*

meditation   A message to go within; seek the still, small voice; the need for a quiet time. *When are you going to start meditating?*

meeting   Work or relationship concerns; getting a group of people together; reaching   common goals;   disagreements;   independence. *Who do you need to meet with to get something settled?*

melt   Relaxation; letting worries go; softening; dissolving or disappearing; merging gradually. *Who is heading for a melt down?*

mend   Needing fixing; something on the mend; getting back your health; repair. *Who needs to mend their ways?*

menu   Choices; planning a dinner party;   check your computer programs;   look at all your options before you decide. *What's on the menu for you?*

Mermaid/merman   Living in a fantasy world; attracted to something out of the ordinary; a sexless person; living in or on the sea.   *Who is acting like a cold fish?*

mess Overwhelmed; liking to mess around with stuff; making a mess of something; a place to eat; a social time; somebody messing with you; cleaning up a mess. *What shouldn't you mess with?*

message A need to communicate; listening to inner messages; inspired words. *Since every dream is a message, what is extra special about this message within a message?*

metal   Unbendable; rigid and cold; precious and rare; being tested; ready to do your best (on one's mettle); full of spirit and courage. (see **medal**) *Who is resistant to change?*

meteor   News from far away; unexpected and surprising; moving at a terrific speed; shooting stars are considered a good omen. *Where have you been receiving messages from unusual sources?*

metronome A need to keep on time; practice makes perfect; repetitious, a musician in your life, time ticking away. *In what activity could you be more regular?*

microfilm   Seeing too many James Bond movies; tiny pictures; making things small and mobile; spying; going to see small movies. *How can you see a bigger picture of yourself?*

microphone   Needing to be heard; no one listening; wanting to be on the stage. *Where do you need to speak up?*

microscope   Picking things apart; looking at tiny details; making things bigger than they are. *What needs to be looked at carefully?*

microwave Quick heating; spending too much time around radiation; operating at a high frequency. *What is agitating you to the point of getting too hot to handle?*

middle Feeling stuck in between;   middle age; middle class, in the middle of something; middle-of-the-road, middle C.   *What are you stuck in the middle of?*

midget   Feeling small; having to look up to others. *What is feeling small in your life?*

military   Strict, regimented; having to fall in line; feeling like a number; at war, obedience; following orders. *How have you ventured off the beaten track?*

milk   Care and nurturance; wanting to be cared for; crying over it; getting all the laughs they can. *Who loves you?*

mill   Repeating the same thing; boredom with daily tasks; wanting a change of scene; getting a lot of experience; learning the hard way; grinding work; a lot of people milling around; a heavy burden. *What can you do to get a fresh perspective?*

millennium   Anticipating big changes; worries about the future and what it might hold; looking forward to a new time. *What feels as if it has taken a thousand years to accomplish?*

mine   Going deep within; getting to the truth; an explosive situation; a mine of information. *What is uniquely yours?*

miniskirt   Showing off; following the latest style; not covered. *What do you really want to show people?*

minister   A person in charge; a friendly ear; acting as a servant or nurse. *Who is in need of ministering?*

miracle   Believing the unbelievable; knowledge not yet scientifically understood; last hope; something wonderful or marvelous. *What miracle are you waiting for?*

mirror   A time to reflect; soul reflection; reflecting truth; identical; a symbol with a long spiritual history; comes from the Latin word meaning wonder; it was believed that when we looked into a mirror, our true self would look back at us. *What would you see now if you were to look into such a magic mirror?*

misfortune Lack of caution; meeting Miss Fortune; believing in bad luck. *What can you learn from the dream misfortune?*

miss   Not quite hitting the mark; an invitation to seize the moment; something not working properly; a young unmarried woman**.** *What is it that you don't want to miss?*

missing   Something missing about to be found; missing someone; something lacking. *What is missing?*

missionary A call to service; giving all you can; finding your mission in life; imposing your beliefs on others**.** *What does your dream tell you about your mission?*

mist   Unable to see what is right in front of you; feeling misty-eyed; something missed; not seeing clearly. *What have you been in a fog about?*

mistake   Feeling bad about something you did; dwelling too long on an error;   make no mistake about it; a difference in opinion. *What could you have done differently?*

mistletoe   Kissing; Christmas kissing; using your toe as a weapon. *What message would your toe give you if it could speak?*

mix Putting things together in a new way; keeping separate; lack of creativity; a good mix; someone mixed up about something.   *What needs to be made clear?*

moat   Feeling surrounded by a strong emotion that either traps or protects; crossing over emotion to get to your castle. *From what do you need protection?*

mob   Losing control; too many people around you; feeling mobbed; part of a gang. *Where are you going along with the mob?*

moccasin   Walking softly on the Earth; appreciation for native ways; knowing how another feels. *Whose moccasins do you need to walk in for awhile?*

model   Trying to be perfect; fearful about setting an example; copying something; shape or fashion an object; displaying yourself.   *Who would you choose to model yourself after?*

mold   Something left aside and neglected; a new shape or form; rich soil. *What part of you needs some attention and cleansing?*

mole   Not getting out enough and meeting new people; living in the dark; spots on the skin; working long and patiently.   *What have you been blind to?*

monastery   A place of peace and quiet; getting away from hectic activity; needing a place of contemplation. (see **monk**) *Who do you know who lives like a monk?*

money   Concerns over finances; look at what is valuable to you; dealing with worthiness issues; valuing what you have. *How much money is enough?*

monitor   Watching life pass you by; keeping track of someone else; check your computer monitor. *How have you been feeling more like an observer in your life instead of an active participant?*

monk   Someone wise and spiritual; living a quiet and protected life; poverty, chastity and obedience, an obsessive compulsive person. (see **monastery**) *Where have you cut yourself off from society?*

monkey Activity and play indicated; something suspicious or not trustworthy; wasting time; full of mischief; copying someone. *How could you take more time to play?*

monster Something feared; getting blown out of proportion; an overactive imagination; a picture of your fears; facing your inner demons; feeling threatened; leading a dull life; a person who is acting monstrous. *What or who might not be as frightening as you have imagined?*

moon spiritual significance; reflection of inner emotional feelings; a twenty-eight day cycle; reflecting the light of another; waxing and a waning; new moon – new beginning; last quarter – completion; a rude joke. *What is your dream moon reflecting to you?*

mop   Cleaning up; a thick head of hair; getting rid of a mess; time to finish something. *What do you need to mop up in your life?*

morning   A new venture; in mourning; Don or Dawn; writing out your dreams. (see **mourning**) *How is morning important to you?*

Morse code   Communication; a special signal sent to you; listen for the message; dreams come in a code; a dotty person; figuring things out. *What is the meaning in the message?*

mosaic An intricate design or pattern; many pieces to make the whole; having to do with Moses; glueing the pieces together. *What details are you missing?*

mosquito Something bugging you; a threat to take away a part of you that you need and value; a stinging female; itching to get away; a high pitched sound. *What is irritating you?*

motel Temporary stay; a visit to a strange place; travel plans; more private than a hotel. *When were you last in a motel and what significance does that have for you now?*

moth Attracted to the light after being in the dark for a while; loving clothes. *What old flame is attracting you?*

mother A female role model; guidance and instruction; nurturance or criticism; acting like your mother. *Who reminds you of your mother?*

motor A dynamo; the thing that makes you go; getting into action; moving quickly. *What makes your motor go?*

mountain Getting to the top; rising on the corporate ladder; spiritual aspiring; making a mountain out of a molehill; a huge amount in front of you; personal challenge. *What is at the top?*

mourning Feeling sad; missing a loved one; after mourning there is a new morning. (see **morning**) *What can you do to say goodbye?*

mouse Someone playing a game with you and chasing you around; a mousy person; quiet as a mouse. *What are you afraid of?*

mouth Speaking your mind; being clear and honest in your communication; feeling low and down in the mouth; getting it from the horse's mouth; someone shooting off their mouth; mouthy; ranting and raving. *Who has just said a mouthful?*

move A change; a time to move on; something new moving in or something old moving out; always on the move; it's your move; moved to tears. *What is the next move?*

movie   Projection of your story; a chance to look at where you've been and where you're going; recent movie seen; a starring role; directing your life. *What title would you give to your life movie?*

movie star   Qualities you admire; bigger than life; fame and fortune; wanting attention; feeling lonely. *Who does your dream star remind you of, or what part of yourself do they symbolize?*

mud   Someone's reputation may be at risk; stuck in one place; needing a change; not clear, time for a facial. *What is muddying up your vision?*

muffler   A need to let off steam; reduce the noise; things heating up; wrapping up warmly. *What are you not saying clearly?*

mug   A tough exterior; big hot drinks, facing something. *Who doesn't like to have their picture taken?*

mule   Feeling like an underdog; working long hours without fair compensation; slopping around the house. *Who is being stubborn?*

mummy   Keeping your mother under wraps; protecting and preserving dead things. (see **mother**) *What will happen if your mother changes?*

mural   A large picture for all to see; many people doing the work; a wall of images. *What picture or subject does your dream self want you to pay attention to?*

murder   Repressed feelings of rage and fear; wanting to murder someone; something very unpleasant, like a murderous job. (see **kill**) *How do the murderer and person who was killed look or seem familiar to you in waking life?*

muscle   Strength; someone trying to muscle their way in; keeping very still; doing too much exercise and getting muscle bound; a weak person. *Who is the muscle man?*

museum Something to be looked at; not used; on display for posterity; a precious relic; historical artifact. *What personal object do you value and why?*

mushroom Growing in a dark, damp place; a nuclear cloud; developing very quickly; fables and fairy tales show mushrooms growing in places that attract spirits and little people. *What fantasy are you wishing for?*

music   Upliftment; writing or making music; singing/dancing; a soul that sings; time to face the music; soothing sounds. *What did the dream music remind you of?*

mustache   Keeping a stiff upper lip; an itchy kisser; a disguise. *Who do you know who wears a mustache?*

mute   Words cannot express how you feel; beyond words; stopping someone else from speaking; talking with your hands. *What are you afraid to say?*

myth   Legend or story about supernatural worlds; a way of explaining origins; a person with a lisp; your own personal tale. *How the does dream myth related to your waking life?*

N

mining the abyss
arcane gold, the mother lode
spilling to the surface
Linda Mazuranic

nail   Hitting it right on; accurate in knowing where to put your energy; an unfeeling person; a nail-biter; nervous; something needing to be attached. *What has come undone for you?*

naked Feeling vulnerable; shy; embarrassed; seeing something clearly with your naked eye. *Where do you feel overly exposed?*

name   Being called names; naming someone; identification; a good reputation; acting for someone else; name-dropping; someone wishing to remain nameless; a namesake. *What's in the name?*

nap   Needing a short rest; caught off guard; napping on the job; a soft velvet cloth. *Where have you been caught napping?*

Napoleon   Acting like a tyrant;   association with France. *Who, or what, in your life is small but mighty?*

narrow A tight squeeze; a narrow escape; a limited opportunity; a narrow mind. *Who needs to be more open minded?*

native Belonging; an aboriginal person; place of origin; going native and living more primitively; Native North American; a person with respect for nature; living with spiritual values; native ability. *What are your native gifts that you are not using?*

nature Authentic; being comfortable with who you are; getting in touch with others; relating to your environment;   not artificial;   made by the Creator rather than humans; qualities you were born with. *What is natural and easy for you that you don't fully appreciate?*

nausea Repressing strong feelings of fear; disgust; perhaps illness indicated; moving too fast; seasickness, or car   sickness; sick of something; pregnancy. *Who is making you sick to your stomach?*

navel   Getting to the centre; being in touch with your gut feelings; an association with the Navy; an old attachment; navel oranges; belly dancer. *What are your gut feelings about a problem or issue?*

Nazi   Evil doings; no respect for life; totalitarianism; not learning from the past; being dominated; cruel and unfeeling.   *How are you being intolerant?*

neck   Something heavy around your neck; finding something hard to swallow; getting it in the neck; in your neck of the woods; sticking your neck out; win by a neck; holding your head up and facing your problem. *What or who is a pain in the neck?*

necklace   A special gift; a lace collar; adorning.   (see **neck**) *What special necklace means a lot to you?*

needle   As difficult as finding a needle in a haystack; woman's work; joining something back together; getting the point; someone being invasive and pressuring you to do something you don't want to do; health issues may be indicated.   *Who is needling you?*

neighbour   Having problems with your workmates or friends; doing a good deed for someone you don't know very well; the person next door. *How does your neighbour remind you of yourself?*

nest   Settling down in one place; wanting to begin a family; getting closer to your own family; being pushed out of the nest too soon; things fitting together neatly; decorating your home. *Who has flown from your nest that you would like back?*

net   Catching something; having a safety net; protection; net income; a fish net; tennis net; hair net; addicted to the Internet. *What has this dream netted for you?*

new   Beginnings; getting a new item or job; someone knew it. *What's new in your life?*

news   Receiving important information; a surprise bit of gossip; encompassing all the directions: north, east, west, south;   look in all directions; waiting for news. *What news do you have to break to someone?*

newspaper   Wanting to be current; keeping up with the latest, new information coming; what happened yesterday is old news.
What are you looking for?

nickname   Not being recognized; being treated as if you aren't important; someone named Nick; shortening your identity; family memories. *How have you been putting yourself down or making light of your accomplishments?*

night   In the dark; making a night of it; a dark secret; a night owl; waiting for your knight;   a time for dreaming; night school. (see **knight**) *What do you like to do at night?*

nightgown   Feeling inappropriately dressed; not having the right thing to wear; embarrassment; sleep. *How can you be better prepared for an upcoming event?*

nightmare   Personal fears; a need for excitement; a way to get your attention; feeling out of control and frightened. *What unpleasantness have you been avoiding?*

nine   A baseball team; a nine-day wonder; having nine lives; having your pins knocked out from under you; saying no; transition number. *What significance is the number nine in your waking life?*

nineteen   A big change coming; the end of a stage in your life. *What new adventure are you moving into this year?*

nipple   needing to be nurtured and nourished; immaturity; being starved of love and affection; possible breast health issue indicated. *How can you better nourish yourself?*

noise   Making a big noise about something; being distracted; not in harmony; wanting attention; a message not coming in clearly. *What is making so much noise that it's making it hard to concentrate?*

noon   Middle time; high noon; twelve o'clock high; lunch time, sun overhead. *What important thing happens at noon?*

noose   Punishment; shame and guilt; getting out of something; feeling trapped into confessing; encircled. *What is your alternative plan if you can't get out of this one?*

north   Cold; frozen; facing the setting sun and turning right; northern lights; a bright star. *What is in the north for you?*

nose   You have a good idea about where to go from here; good instincts; someone knows; count noses and be sure all are here; someone being led by the nose; looking down one's nose at someone; something right on the nose; paying through the nose; putting someone's nose out of joint; turning up your nose at something; right under your nose; search something out; taking a nose-dive. *Who is being nosey?*

note   Keeping track; part of a song; hitting the right note; a note of anxiety or excitement; compare notes with someone; make a note so you won't forget; a conspicuous person; a noteworthy even. *Who do you need to drop a note to?*

notebook   Writing your life story; keeping close records of what is going on at work or at school; keeping a dream journal. *What have you missed writing about?*

novel   Unusual; a long story; the story of your life; new; strange. *What novel has made an impact on you?*

numb   Cutting off feelings; shutting down emotionally; health issues may be indicated; dull; having no feeling. *What past pain are you reluctant to feel?*

number   Look at where your dream number appears in waking life: license plate, house, phone, age, etc;   something beyond number; a book in the Old Testament; someone afraid their number is up; addicted to counting things or keeping track. *Who is number one?*

nun   Teaching; healing; spiritual practices of women; seeing things in black and white. *Are you walking the talk?*

nurse   Care and attention; possible medical concerns; getting well; nursing old wounds; feeding a baby. *How can you take better care of yourself?*

nut   The centre of the issue; the beginning of a new project; a hard nut to crack. *Who has been acting nutty?*

Lost amidst your lifetimes dreaming
worlds where neither wing nor hoof
flits nor tramples — void of meaning
worlds to wonder — dreams enough

Jan 29, 1987

Ruth Cunningham

O

oak   strong, resilient;   persevering; a history of determination and strength; long living; coming from small things. *How can your past history of moving through adversity help you now?*

oar   Moving forward on your own steam; strength and physical exertion; time to take a rest on your oars. *What alternatives might you consider before making your final decision?*

oasis   Needing a rest; a time-out away from daily pressures, camels; desert. *How can you make a safe and harmonious retreat for yourself right where you are?*

oats   Needing comfort and kindness; more dietary fibre may be indicated; sowing wild oats. *Who is feeling their oats?*

obesity   Worries about weight and appearance; fear of social rejection; being overly concerned about weight; fears. (see **fat**) *What problem is an overweight condition covering up?*

obey   Following the rules; rebellious; protesting the way things are done; being young and full of energy; feeling pressured to conform; old marriage vows. *What are you choosing to obey?*

object   A symbol of a part of yourself; someone objecting; being treated as an object. *In what way does the appearance and function of the dream object remind you of yourself, or your lifestyle?*

observe   Watching yourself; feeling disconnected; possibly precognitive; may be a warning dream. *What are you not noticing in your waking life that is prominent in your dream?*

obstacle   Something in your way; feeling trapped; frustration. *How is the dream obstacle familiar to your waking life?*

ocean   Unpredictable, mother relationship may be indicated; issues with mother seem overwhelming; new information about your abilities and potential;   an important dream symbol that signifies a vital message;   relationship with inner self reflected in the state of the dream ocean;   being connected to an encompassing and life-giving source; representing the unconscious that holds many treasures; notice if your ocean is calm, turbulent, cold, or wavy. (see **sea & see**) *What is constantly flowing in and out of your life?*

octagon   Something eight-sided; the shape of a stop sign; there are many angles to look at; the eighth something – day, month, year. *What was taken away one October?*

octopus   Feeling smothered; pulled into something undesirable; somebody all over you like an octopus; an organization that has far-reaching influences; a big hug. *What do you keep reaching for?*

odour   Strong memory; nostalgia, something stinky. *What does the odour in the dream remind you of?*

offering   A need for giving service to others; giving stuff away. *What has been offered to you lately?*

office   Work concerns indicated; acting indifferent or cold and businesslike; overworked. *Who is working too much overtime?*

officer   A commanding presence; being ordered about; a policeman; feelings of guilt; authority figure. *Who is in charge?*

officials   Feeling watched or criticized;   judged; threatened with punishment; being shown the right way. *Who's the big cheese?*

ogre   Being bullied; treated like a bug; pushed around; scary person. *Who is the bully?*

oil   Financial abundance indicated; slippery deal that could pay off big; making things calm and peaceful. *Who's being slick?*

ointment   Getting stuck; trapped; feeling unable to make choices; one little problem might stop the whole project. *Who needs a salve for a skin problem?*

old   Overdue; overstaying your welcome; concerns about aging; familiar. *What's getting old for you?*

olive   Making peace with someone; sourness; Greek or Italian may be indicated. *Who is offering you an olive branch as a symbol of apology or forgiveness?*

Olympic   Feeling under pressure to perform; challenge and competition indicated; doing your best; going for the big one. *Where are you giving your all?*

omelette   Feeling as if you revealed too much, too early; feeling intellectually vulnerable; high cholesterol.   *How can you mix something together in a new and creative way?*

one   Needing to be first; alone; feeling whole and complete; in numerology one is individuation, independence and attainment. *Who is number one in your life?*

onions   Feeling teary, sad, confused; many layers to an issue;   look deeper within. *How can you cleanse yourself of some old patterns and start over from a fresh place?*

opera A big drama happening; making sounds; witnessing a moving event. *Who is raising their voice with great emotion?*

operation   A need to take action; taking the problem apart to find the root cause; planning your moves carefully.   *What can be fixed by removing the problem area, or tying some loose ends together?*

operator   A person who manoeuvers people for their own use; taking charge. *Who is the smooth operator?*

opponent   Anger, frustration and competitiveness may be indicated. *How does your opponent   reveal qualities that you find difficult to accept in yourself?*

opposite   Thinking and making decisions in extremes; finding a balance; look another way at something.   *What or who is opposing you?*

optical   Unable to see properly; missing important details.   *What situation do you need to look at more closely?*

orange   Social colour;   not getting enough liquids; needing to brighten up; warmth; morning time. *How could you be more sociable?*

orchestra   Hearing the music; making music together; a relaxing leisure activity; working together in harmony. *How are you cooperating with others for a pleasing outcome?*

orchid   Rare and exotic; needing warmth and care; expensive date. *How are you different from the usual?*

organ   Solitary activity; church music; might refer to your lungs and how well air is being pumped through them; check out your internal organs. *What are some ways to inspire yourself?*

orgy   Sexual deprivation; time to get out and have some fun. *How could you express your sexuality in ways that are safe and satisfying?*

Orient   Exotic, unusual, spicy; mysterious; something eastern. *How can you put a little spice into your life?*

ornament   A need to add some beauty to your life; extra; not essential; Christmas. *What part of yourself is for decoration only?*

orphan   Loneliness; isolation; feeling that you don't belong; wanting your mother or father. *What is missing in your life that you need to adopt?*

Oscar   Needing approval; deserving the top award. *What big performance do you want to be recognized for?*

ostrich   Ignoring a problem; moving swiftly; can't get off the ground. *What or who are you hiding from?*

otter   Taking time to relax and have fun; swimming around in the unconscious can be quite enjoyable; playful. *What is it that you 'ottah' do?*

Ouija board   Predicting the future for fun; asking difficult questions; wondering what is in store for you. *Where in your life are you answering yes and no at the same time?*

out   Outside; in the open air; out of sight; on the outs with someone; outbursts; feeling like an outcast; down and out; three strikes, you're out; getting out from under; having a new outlook; feeling out-numbered. *What new outlet is your dream suggesting?*

outhouse   Functioning naturally out of doors; wanting to get out of the house. *Who is put out?*

ovary   Creativity; full of potential; may indicate a physical problem; new beginnings. *When do you say, "oh, very?"*

oven **G**etting hot; cooked; overdone; on the hot seat; going through a profound change; womb. *What is heating up in your life?*

overboard   Losing your balance; plunging into the unconscious, or your emotions; going to extremes; being bored. *What are you ready to throw away?*

overflow   Extra, unnecessary, redundant; too much; flooding; abundant. *When do you feel like the extra person?*

owl   Night person; associated with wisdom, age, good advice. *What have you learned from your dream owl?*

owner Possessions, to take ownership; identifying with your possessions. *What are you afraid of losing?*

P

full moon stared at me
daring me to dance free
shining through my fear
Linda Mazuranic

pad   Writing; guarding body parts; a place to take off from; wanting a place of your own. *Who pads on quiet feet?*

paddle   Leaving by boat; punishment; slow means of transportation; wading right into something. *Who is up the creek without a paddle?*

padlock   Locked up tight; safety issues indicated. *What have you locked away?*

page   Time to turn over a new leaf; reading or writing something important; a young boy; summoned or called for. *From whose book of life would you like to read a page?*

pail   Not feeling well (a pale face); carrying a load; needing more colour in your life. *Who is acting outside the bounds of acceptable behaviour?*

pain   Health issues indicated; tolerating too much discomfort without seeking a way to ease it; someone being a pain; something missing; feeling overloaded. *What could your pain be teaching you?*

paint   Covering up; hiding a flaw; a fresh start; a part of your life that needs restoring; expressing your creativity; makeup. *What could do with a fresh coat of paint?*

painting   Artistic expression indicated; capturing a life event for posterity; painting the dream would be a learning exercise; creative inspiration. *Who is painting the town red?*

pair   Wanting to find a partner; spending too much time alone; two of something. (see **pear**) *What pair are you a part of?*

palace   Desire for wealth; feeling deprived; wanting more out of life; learning from one's past; a movie palace. *Who is the queen or king in your life?*

palette   Having a range of colours available; not following your artistic leanings; painting a picture. *How can you make your life more colourful and exciting?*

palm   Palm Sunday; a welcome; greasing someone's palm; being open-handed; having an itching palm; palm something off; a hot date. *Who needs a hand up?*

palm tree Tropical holiday; seeing a psychic; seeking forgiveness. *Who is going south soon?*

pan   A belief in fairies; cooking; leaping the fire; hoping for a change due to uncomfortable feelings; hoping things will pan out all right; taking in the whole scene; panhandling. *Where, or when, have you been on the hot seat?*

panda Reminder of childhood panda bear; a police car; eating greens. *What are you seeing in black and white?*

panic   Worry; focusing on one thing; may indicate a concern to check out. *What fear are you suppressing?*

pansy   Feeling shy about doing something; fear about your masculinity. *Who has put a brave face on?*

pants   Covering up your private parts; wearing the pants in the family; out of breath. *What are you panting to do?*

pantyhose Confinement; conformity; feeling inappropriately dressed; wanting to cover up a part of you that needs more freedom to move. *Who's all dressed up and has nowhere to go?*

paper   Message by fax or mail; swamped with paperwork; reading something significant in the newspaper; documents needing to be signed; busy as a one-handed paper hanger; a paper due. *What do you need to write down?*

paper bag   Temporary container; a simple lunch; old fashioned values; hiding something. *What are you carrying around?*

parachute   Needing an escape; wanting to get out of something safely; folding carefully. *What equipment do you need to land safely?*

parade   Celebration; showing off your accomplishments; a holiday. *Who is raining on your parade?*

paradise   Wanting to get away; a belief in an after life; not liking where you are; a perfect place to live. *What situation would feel like paradise to you?*

paralysis   Feeling stuck; frozen to the spot; feeling confined; something stopping you from moving forward; your mind waking up before your body. *Where do you feel helpless to move?*

parcel   A surprise package arriving; time to wrap something up; a piece of land; a gift. *What gift can you give yourself?*

parent   Being treated like a child; in need of guidance and nurturing; listening to your supportive and wise inner parent; feeling guilty and watched. *What is now apparent that you have missed?*

park   Staying in one place for a while; enjoying the environment; time to walk and enjoy the beauty of nature; leisure time. *Where you do park yourself for comfort?*

parking lot   Waiting for something to happen; shopping; office; doing a lot of parking; temporary stay; paying your own way. *Who sits around a lot and does nothing?*

parking ticket   Stopping in the wrong place; staying too long; not paying what you owe; needing permission to stay. *Who is in the wrong place at the wrong time?*

parrot   Associated with prophecy; a gaudy chatterer; repetition; copying; following the crowd; looking for Paradise. *Who is going along with everyone else?*

part Leaving someone or something; doing your share; taking something apart; having a piece; do your part; feeling as if you are falling apart. *What do you not want to part with?*

partner   Joining with another part of yourself; sharing with someone; a spouse; significant other; wanting a partner. *Where can you ask for help when you need it?*

party   Time to relax and see a few friends; feeling pressured by a lot of people; political party; someone being a party pooper; the life of the party. *What are you party to now?*

passenger   Not willing to take the controls; going along for the ride; paying your way. *Who is driving you around?*

passion   a reminder about what you love to do; high energy; strong attraction to another; needing to make a change; desire. *What do you feel passionate about?*

passport   Taking a holiday in a different country; needing legal permission to go somewhere; going past a port. *Whose permission do you need to get in order to go your own way?*

pastry   Abundance; riches; luxuries; a tart; not taken seriously; mother's pie. *How can you indulge yourself in a few luxuries?*

pasture   Taking it easy; taking some time off; something growing; whipping things together; being put out to pasture; reference to horses. *Who needs to eat more greens?*

pat   Someone giving you a pat answer; a pat on the back; playing children's games (pat-a-cake); holding your ground and standing pat; someone named Pat. *Whose feathers have been ruffled and now need patting?*

patch   Repairing a relationship; covering something up to keep it going for a little while longer; a small piece of ground just for you; doing things in a patch work fashion; something inferior to your standard; a quilt. *What needs patching up?*

path   Following a prescribed route; venturing off the traditional way; thinking of your life's path; being guided; a blocked path; a new way offered; wherever you are is your path. *How can you get back on your desired path?*

patient Taking care of someone; can't wait for something to happen; feeling anxious. *What could you do while you are waiting?*

pattern   Doing the same old thing in the same old way; a new way to do it; an ideal to follow; time to redecorate your house. *What new pattern would you like to have?*

pauper   Fear or shame of being poor; not giving all you can. *What female do you feel like popping in the nose?*

pavement   Hard; unrelenting; long lasting; immutable; playing hop scotch or roller skating. *What might cushion your fall?*

paw Feeling invaded by a beastly person; unprotected; vulnerable and instinctive; your dad; time to slow down and pause. *Who is trying to get their paws on you?*

pawnshop   In need of a loan; security issues; being treated as unimportant; feeling undervalued. *What are you in risk of losing for short term pleasure?*

pay   Owing someone; something owed to you; having to pay your own way; taking revenge; pay back time; waiting for pay-day; consider the pay off; pay your respects to someone. *What is costing you too much?*

peace   Too much fighting going on; a piece of something; trying to keep the peace; time to make a peace offering and ask for forgiveness; make time to meditate. *Who do you need to make peace with?*

peach   Linked with spring, youth, marriage and protective magic; peach blossoms are emblems of purity; warm and fuzzy; juicy; a peach of a person; soft skin. *Who is soft on the outside, but hard at their core?*

peacock   Symbol of royalty; also of rebirth; associated with the sin of pride; showing off your colours and beauty; feeling proud or shy. *Who is strutting their stuff?*

peak   Reaching a goal; getting all you desire; the climax to a long period of struggling; having a peek at something; someone who wears a peaked cap. (see **peek**) *What are you working toward that seems a long way off?*

pear   Mother or love symbol; pear shaped; juicy fruit.   (see **pair**) *What do you need to pare down?*

pearl   Symbol of femininity; spiritual wisdom, wealth; the centre of beauty; the heart of the matter;   a woman named Pearl; a symbol for the moon; giving something to someone who doesn't appreciate it; an irritant that, over time, changes into something valuable; pearls of wisdom. *Who gave up before reaching the treasure?*

pebble   Some small thing annoying you; a visit to the beach; something bumpy. *Who thinks they can't be replaced?*

pedal   Working hard to get somewhere in a hurry; working on your own without support; a need to put your foot down, bicycling. (see **petal**) *What are you trying to peddle?*

pedestal   Looking up to someone; putting yourself down. *Who have you put on a pedestal?*

peek   Needing a better look at something; seeing something you shouldn't. (see **peak**) *What are you looking for?*

peel   Stripping away the outer layer; settling for the covering without going deeper. *Who is focusing on their outer appearance, while not realizing their inner qualities?*

peg   Something needs fastening; feeling hung out to dry; Peg or Margaret; washday. *Who need to be taken down a peg?*

pen   Writing a letter to someone you love; doing something by hand; old fashioned; careful; paying attention to detail; writing out your dreams; feeling penned in; associated with jail.   *Who   lives in a pig pen?*

pencil   drawing; a thing of the past that you can erase; childhood drawing. *What part of you needs sharpening?*

pen pal   A writing friend; wanting to communicate; pals with your pens. *Who haven't you written to for a long time?*

penis   May indicate health problems; sexual desire; needing to move away from a pushy person. *Who did the penis in the dream belong to and how do you feel about this person or that part of his anatomy?*

penny   Feeling poor; money issues; honesty; being penny wise and pound foolish; lucky penny. *What is costing you a pretty penny?*

pentagram   Symbol of harmony; health and mystic powers; with one point up and two down, it is the sign of white magic; with two points up, it signifies the devil's horns, and evil. *What significance does five have in your life?*

people   Represent different parts of yourself; qualities you like and don't like about yourself; too many people around.   *What are your dream people showing you about yourself?*

pepper   hot and spicy; needing a change. *What is coming at you strong and fast?*

perfect   Not feeling good enough; having all its parts. *Who thinks they are perfect?*

perform   Feeling judged; doubting your own abilities; acting; doing something against your will. *What if you stop performing?*

perfume   Adorning yourself; going to a party; covering up; wanting the nice things in life; a stinky person. *What isn't smelling too sweet to you?*

periscope   The subconscious having a peek to see if it's safe to emerge; taking an emotional viewpoint; looking around corners. *How is what-you-see a mirror reflecting what you are not seeing about yourself?*

permanent   Having a bad hair day; wanting something to last; feeling insecure; holding on to your thoughts. *What did you think was permanent but turned out not to be?*

pervert   Something used in the wrong way; changing inappropriately; abnormal sexual practice caused by repressed sexuality. *What natural instincts are being repressed and perverted?*

pet   A comforting friend; missing a pet; a pet name; pet theory; teacher's pet. *Who needs some tender loving care?*

petal   Something delicate; wondering if she/he loves you or not. (see **pedal**) *What special flower have you saved?*

petroglyph   Ancient wisdom; old messages; something told in pictures; carved or painted on rocks.   *What feels as if it has been written in stone?*

pew   Feeling guilty because you haven't been to church; something stinks; a hard place to sit. *What do you need to meditate on?*

pharmacy   Health concerns may be indicated; interaction of various drugs; filling a prescription. *What did you buy at the pharmacy lately?*

phone Communicate before it is too late; speak up; listen to someone special.   (see **telephone**) *When or where   do you need to listen to yourself talking?*

photograph   Something developing; a picture of health; kept for posterity; not looking at the negative; perceiving an issue from   two dimensions; acting like a phony; remembering by gone days. *Who is not getting the picture?*

physician Health concerns may be indicated; paying attention to physical signs and symptoms of health issues.   (see **doctor**) *What is being doctored?*

piano   Being played with; culture; sophistication; in harmony; many keys to choose from; a black and white issue; sweet music. *What tune does your piano play?*

pickle   Confusion; worry and problems that seem insurmountable; sour; bitterness and preservation may be indicated; a picnic. *Who is in a pickle now?*

picnic Enjoyment; leisure time; taking time to enjoy yourself; summertime. *What is no picnic for you?*

picture   Get all the facts before you make a decision; a likeness to someone else; visualization may be helpful; feeling framed or on show; pouring as in pitcher. *How can you achieve a clearer picture of the situation?*

pie   Homey; something real easy; homespun; a reminder of earlier times; a pie in the sky idea; deep baked; covered with dough. *Where do you feel you are not getting your full share?*

pig   Intelligent animal; often associated with overeating, bad manners and aggression; laziness, ignorance and being closed minded; buying a pig in a poke; gluttony; ancient symbol of the Great Mother; saving money in a piggy bank; over-indulging; in Chinese philosophy the pig represents masculine strength. *Who has been acting like a pig?*

pigeon   Stuck in a pigeon hole; having twins; toes that turn in; someone making a mess of things; a lot of cooing going on. *Who has a special message for you?*

pill   Medical problem may be indicated; someone behaving in an irritating manner; information that is hard to swallow; forgetting to take your pills. *Who is the real pill in your life?*

pillar   Strength; longevity; tall; standing your ground; having a good reputation; over-estimating a strength; someone going from pillar to post; support. *Who is a pillar of your community?*

pillow   Being comfortable; needing more rest; having a soft place to land; working with dreams; a feather head; unimportant person. *Who is your pillow?*

pilot   On course; operating the controls; a guide or leader; a new beginning; a small light always burning; piling stuff around. *Who is at the controls?*

pin   Feeling pinned down; holding something together; a special pin to wear; getting the point; knocked off your pins; on pins and needles; a pin head; a pin-up; needing some pin money. *What do you need to pinpoint before going forward?*

pinch   Someone treating you badly; filling-in in an emergency; taking something with a pinch of salt; doing something because you feel you have to. *Who is feeling the pinch when it comes to money?*

pine   A person who never learns and is always green;   you have grieved long enough; a tree lover. *Who are you waiting for?*

pink   Monetary windfall; a colour often associated with females; beauty; attractiveness; spring; someone with radical political views; a fancy edging; trouble with your little pinkie; motherhood.   *Who is feeling 'in the pink'?*

pipe   Birth; emergence; being reborn; sacred smoke; pipes of pan or bagpipes; oil; someone needs to pipe down; being piped aboard a new vessel; someone with pipe dreams; a need to smoke the peace pipe; quiet contemplation; far out surfing; someone who smokes a pipe. *What is coming down the pipeline for you?*

piranha   Being eaten alive; feeling attacked from all sides. *Who is viciously nibbling at you?*

pistol   Violence; taking a pot shot; being on target with your goals; feeling defensive. *Who are you secretly angry at?*

pit   Falling; depressed and feeling trapped; need cheering up; the cheap seats; time for a pit-stop to refuel; pitting your strength against another; a hard seed; be careful of the pitfalls; making music unseen. *What are the pits in your life?*

pizza   European descent; Italian ancestry; lots of toppings; quick and easy food. *Who is acting like a teenager?*

plane   Flying high; a trip or vacation may be indicated; feeling out of control; on the level; a need to smooth things out; easy to understand; ordinary. *What do you need to say in plain language?*

planet Wholeness and awareness; taking in the big picture; ecologically conscious; check out your horoscope. *How can you help the planet today?*

planetarium   Some of your ideas are out of this world; stars in your eyes; looking up too long. *Who is the stargazer?*

plant   New ideas; a place of work; a scheme to trap or mislead; a person who can trick you; set firmly in place; hold your ground. *What, or who, needs replanting?*

plastic   Unnatural; long-lasting; easily impressionable; acting phony. *Who wants to have plastic surgery?*

plate   Eating; getting nourishment; feeling a little flat; a dish in your life; covered with armour; home base; covered with a thin layer. *Where have you got too much on your plate?*

play   Not enough play; suspecting foul play; feeling played-out; playing into the hands of someone; playing it out to the end; putting on a good act; playing up to someone; playing back a scene; always look for a play on words in your dreams; playing down an important matter; feeling like a plaything. *Who is trying to take advantage of you by playing upon your feelings?*

playboy   Possibly a cover up for insecurity; a magazine with good articles; throwing off controls and inhibitions; sexuality. *Who is not ready to commit to a relationship?*

playground   Feeling youthful; happy; memories of a carefree time; acting too seriously. *Who is all work and no play?*

plough   Working hard to get through something; tired and bored with the same old thing; time to reinvest; feeling overwhelmed; dig deep and turn over new soil; male fertility symbol; labour. *What issue are you ploughing through?*

plumbing   Health concerns may be indicated; passing water; a spiritual insight; something needs o be flushed out; blocking your feelings; check the plumbing in your body and in your house. *What is going down?*

pocket   Secret and private place; having a secret about money or identity; feeling isolated; out of pocket, as in spending or losing money; stealing. *What are you trying to get away with?*

point   An important issue pointed out to you; someone being directive and guiding; get the point; look at your good points; you are on the point of doing something; something that's beside the point; someone trying to make a point; get to the point; at point blank range; something pointless; a new point of view. *What is pointing you in a new direction?*

poison   A toxic situation or person; a poison-pen letter; turned off by something. *What are you taking in that is poison to your body or soul?*

police   Symbol of authority; feeling oppressed; afraid of punishment; keeping order; difficulty in keeping a commitment; being reckless. (see **cop**) *How are you unnecessarily on guard?*

pond   Calm emotions; a smaller issue to deal with; something heavy and ponderous; something making ripples on the surface. (see **water**) *What do you need to ponder?*

poodle   Being pampered; cared for; indulgence; superficial beauty; fickle; moody; pet dog. *Who is acting spoiled and pampered?*

pool   Enclosing or containing your emotions, or unconscious; needing exercise; pooling your resources; a car pool; playing the pools. *Who is behind the eight ball?*

popcorn   A corny dad; taking life too seriously; watching others live exciting lives instead of doing so yourself; all puffed up; a movie lover. *How can you get more fibre into your diet?*

possession   Owning something; being yours to give or keep; not wanting to share; an emphasis on material goods; representing status. *Who is impressed with their own toys?*

post   Receiving or sending a letter; aftermath of a big event; could indicate depression; the start of a big race; support; putting up a notice; on duty; being called to your quarters; a new assignment; putting a date off until the future.   *What item do you need to enter into the ledger of your life?*

pot   Going to pot; heat changes things; a potbelly; something gambled; a lot of money; marijuana; trying to keep the pot boiling; someone getting potted; taking pot luck. *Who is looking for the pot of gold?*

potato   An old standby; something underground; a buried treasure; passivity; waiting for something to come to you; hard work needed to dig up what you must know *Who is the couch potato?*

pothole   Falling; getting stuck; an unexpected problem in the road ahead; a leaky pot. *What pothole of life do you stumble over?*

poultice   Salve; surface healing; health issue related to skin or lung congestion may be indicated. *What ingredients in your dream poultice might help with a body problem you are having?*

pour   Things flowing easily; pouring your emotions out; someone pouring it on. *What are you getting too much of?*

pray   Seeking or needing divine guidance; a humbling experience; someone who doesn't have a prayer; being hunted, or hunting; something preying on your mind. *What are you praying to have happen, or not happen?*

precognition   Knowing ahead of time what is going to happen; a warning; a way to be prepared;   a gift of prophecy.   *What are you being shown that you can still change?*

pregnancy   Pregnancy may be indicated; expecting; waiting for a big event; full of yourself; a silence full of meaning. *Who, or what, is pregnant with promise?*

prehistoric   Old history returning; something from your past may be resurfacing; early childhood; something instinctive. *Who is acting like a prehistoric animal?*

president   In love with power; needing assistance from a person you believe to be powerful; resembles a president; leaders in dreams represent collective power, control, authority, wisdom, knowledge and guidance. *Who wants to be president?*

pressure   Too much stress; feeling pushed under; relaxation is important; a pressure-cooker situation. *Where are you expecting too much of yourself?*

price   Something costing more than you are willing to pay; paying a heavy price; beyond price; extremely valuable. *What do you want at any price?*

priest Religious figure; symbol of wisdom, kindness, non materialistic values, forgiveness; needing to talk to a nonjudgmental, objective person. *What wise counsel is your dream priest giving you?*

prince   Privilege; having it all; huge inheritance; getting the best of everything; a real neat guy; luxury;   shadow side is the prince of darkness; heroic; gentle; tired of kissing frogs; an ideal young man. *Who do you envy for having it all?*

princess   Time to value your feminine side; being pampered; spoiled; always getting your own way; virginity; feeling special; an ideal young woman; wanting a softer mattress or life. *Who is daddy's little princess?*

principal   Very important; someone giving orders; getting a lot of interest; expecting someone else to act for you; a fundamental truth; honour; a method of operation; memories of school. *Who do you admire for their high principles?*

print   Making an impression; check your printer; back up your work; a need to return to the simplicity of childhood; something you value that is out of print; a repeating design; not the original. *What printed work has made an impression on you?*

prison   Repressed; doing something you don't want to do; seeking the approval of others; a need for self-control; a prisoner of love; not free to be yourself; something needs to be locked up. *Who, or what, is holding you prisoner?*

prize   Winning; getting everything you want; getting the recognition you deserve for all your hard work. *What do you prize?*

professor Being instructed; returning to school; wisdom; intelligence; professing something. *What knowledge do you seek?*

projector   Movie goer, putting on others what is in yourself; throwing or pushing something forward. *Who has qualities that you don't like, but which are similar to yours?*

propeller   Going around in circles; feeling propelled to do something; moving forward; ceiling fan. *Where are you going round and round but getting nowhere?*

prophet   A special inner figure; wise counsel; spiritual guidance; forgiveness; dreams of prophets are very special; pay attention to the wise advice and the feeling you had when seeing the prophet; consider what actions you are inspired to do upon awakening; this might be a turning point for you, one you may remember for the rest of your life. *What changes are you inspired to make happen for yourself?*

prostitute   Selling yourself for less than you deserve; making deals that leave you feeling unappreciated and used; feeling naughty; working at something you hate. *In what way are you selling yourself?*

prune   Constipation or other health issue may be indicated; lack of liquids; dried up like a prune; possibly aging problems; cutting out useless or undesirable parts. *What needs pruning from your life?*

psychiatrist   Someone to listen;   may symbolize your own inner psychiatrist, advising you about a psychological problem that needs attention. *What is the psychiatrist saying or doing in the dream that could help you?*

psychologist Wondering what makes you tick; interested in the mind and how it works; feeling tested; look at your behaviour and feelings about a specific issue. *What have you been trying to figure out, and what further clues has your dream given you?*

puddle Something spilled; childhood memories of splashing through puddles; nature's mirror. *What is your dream showing you to look at in yourself?*

pull Trying hard to get something; pulling something apart; giving help to others; pull over and check things out; pull it off successfully; get out from under; get it together. *Who wants to pull up stakes and make a big move?*

pump Needing help to get up; feeling depressed and sad may be indicated; trying to get information from someone; wearing uncomfortable shoes to please others. *Who needs pumping up?*

pumpkin Fall season; childhood memories; Thanksgiving; harvest time; feeling ghoulish; trying on a different face. *If the Jack-o-lantern could speak to you, what would it say?*

punishment Feelings of guilt and shame; deserving punishment for a wrong-doing; time to reflect on forgiveness; being too hard on yourself. *Who is being a little harsh?*

purple Special color symbolizing royalty, or spirituality; may indicate bruising, pain, or desire to run away; turning purple with rage; aiming high; don't wait until you are old to wear it. *How might your dream be pointing out something very special?*

purse Keeping personal effects safe; a change in identity; money worries; having some privacy; tighten or loosen the purse-strings; possibly coming into some money. *What was happening to the purse* *in your dream that feels familiar in relation to money or identity in your life?*

push   Feeling like a push over; being pushed too far; time to do some push ups; a pushy person. *What are you feeling pushed to do?*

puzzle   Confusion; feelings of inadequacy and frustration; something to puzzle out; putting the pieces together.   *What are you puzzled about?*

pyjamas   Unsuitably dressed for the occasion; feeling exposed; needing to get more rest. *Who do you know who wears pyjamas?*

pyramid   An ancient symbol of the creative power of the Sun; mortality; catching the light; protecting secrets; eternal matters; stability; mystical powers; one of the Seven Wonders of the World; costs gradually increasing; bottom-heavy.   *Where does a pyramid appear in your life?*

"A dream is a condensed reflection
of our existence."

Fritz Perls

Q

a healing nightmare;
embracing the madwoman
two becoming one
Nora Leonard

quake Expecting the worst; shaking with fear; living in an earthquake zone. *What has shaken your world?*

quarrel Anger at someone; afraid to be honest about disagreeing with people; fear of argument; sadness. *With whom would you like to make amends?*

quart Measurement; four glasses; association with milk. *Who is measuring out their love?*

quarter Twenty-five percent; two bits; short of money; uncomfortable with someone at close quarters. *Who is doing a quarter of the work?*

quartz Hard as stone; a friend who loves crystals; tuning in; special spiritual significance symbolizing the inner self; shiny; making rainbows. *Who has a lot of quartz crystals?*

queen A woman leader; the centre; things come easily to this woman; beautiful, strong and mighty; powerful and able to move straight or diagonal. *Who's the Queen Bee?*

quick A nimble Jack; pressure to perform; a need to work faster; wanting a quick fix; a quick-witted person. *Who is moving too quickly for you?*

quicksand   Feeling overwhelmed; drowning; sinking fast; being sucked in. *What are you getting mired in?*

quill Sharp, pointed remarks; writings from the past; a need to defend yourself; writing a letter to your dream self. *Who do you need to write a letter to?*

quilt Warm, cozy; memories of childhood; feeling at home and safe; many pieces making up a whole; connection to family history; a sewing circle. *How are you connecting with a group of like-minded women?*

quit   Finishing something; time to stop; enough is enough; seeing the end in sight. *What are you having trouble quitting?*

quiz   Asking for help; finding the right answer; not knowing all the answers. *What question do you want answered?*

"As you record more dreams,
you will remember more dreams."
Stephen La Berge

R

*midnight dream prowler
shapeshifting into the
bark of a fox
Nora Leonard*

rabbit   Frightened; innocent; sweet and childlike; pregnancy test; soft motherly connection; liking lettuce. *Who is running fast?*

race   Competition; getting ahead of the crowd; feeling harried and busy. *Who is still in the running?*

radio   Unable to turn down the outer noise; not having control over the talk going on inside your head; a voice-message may be indicated; give yourself permission to say what you need to; communication and freedom of speech. *What announcement are you ready to make?*

raft   Feeling adrift; cut off from friends and family; adventurous; survival issues. *Who is just floating along?*

rage   Repressed anger; frustration; feeling overwhelmed. *Who, or what, are you so mad about?*

rags   Inappropriate dress; not confident about your clothes; feeling self-conscious about a financial situation; a poor person; cleaning up; from rags to riches. *In what area of your life do you feel insecure?*

rail   Following the beaten track; conforming to society's norms; no choice; complaining; straight and narrow. *Who would like to ride the rails?*

rain   Lacking moisture; things coming at you thick and fast; a time for refreshing; a blessing from heaven; hiding under your umbrella; pull in the reins; taking a rain-check; feeling ruled by another. *Who is holding the reins?*

rainbow   A big reward at the end; wishing for things to change; a heavenly bridge. *What are you waiting for over the rainbow?*

rake   A flirty man; digging things up; the end of a stage in your life; letting things end in season. *What are you raking in?*

ram   Born under the sign of Aries; strength; virility; protector; getting through, no matter what. *What do you need to stand up to?*

Rambo   Macho man; a man who takes charge; bullying; getting his way through violence. *Who is acting like Rambo?*

ramp   An incline or decline; needing a lift; a disability. *Who needs to get off the highway of life and settle down?*

rape   Feeling overpowered; violated – verbally, emotionally, or physically; fear of sex and violence; a type of grain; unable to defend yourself. *Who is taking advantage of you?*

rash   Acting impulsively; not giving it a lot of thought; being too hasty; a message to think before you act; sensitive skin. *Who is acting rashly so that you feel rushed?*

rat   Gossip; telling malicious stories about people to authority figures; being sneaky, unpredictable and predatory; somebody smells a rat; living in a sewer; fed up with it all; a vermin in your life. *Who is ratting on you?*

raven　　Black; delirious and frenzied; important symbol for the aboriginal peoples of North America. (see **crow**) *To what, or whom, do you need to say "nevermore"?*

razor　Sharp; cutting remarks; on the edge; having your power taken away; needing a shave. *Who is taking a piece out of you?*

read　　Gathering information; not comprehending; reading between the lines; reading more into something than is necessary; being well-read. (see **reed**) *Whose mind would you like to read?*

recipe　Following instructions; know the ingredients of what you are eating; memories of home. *What is your recipe for happiness?*

record　　Keeping track of important information; making notes of your actions; listening to the same things over and over; breaking a record; saying something off the record; going on record. *Who is repeating themselves?*

red　　Bright, passionate sexual love; anger; high emotion; physical; losing money; red blooded; rolling out the red carpet; waving a red flag; throwing in a red herring; a red letter day; stop and look at what you are doing; cutting through the red tape; finishing a lot of books; well read. *What part of your life is red hot?*

reed　　Swamped with work; breathing through a tube. (see **read**) *Whose boat (life) is getting caught up in the reeds?*

refrigerator　In cold storage; keeping things preserved for future use; a cool person; preservation; time to cool down. *How are you being left out in the cold?*

regret　Sadness; guilt about past actions; wishing you had done things differently. *When are you going to forgive yourself for being human?*

rein   Keeping a tight rein; time to draw in the reins; giving more rein to someone; changing directions. (see **rain**) *Who is controlling you?*

relative   Intimacy; family and kinship ties; relationships that have a history; seeing things from another perspective. *Who does the dream relative remind you of?*

religion   Organized worship; following prescribed rules of conduct; getting that old time religion; spirituality. *What beliefs are you questioning?*

remote control   Distancing yourself; controlling at arm's length. *Whose turn is it at the controls?*

remove   Taking away a piece of your life; an important thing altered in some way; loss; time to get out of there. *What are you removing yourself from, and why?*

rent   A temporary stay; lack of commitment; short term; borrowing from someone; paying your dues; tearing something apart. *What are you renting?*

repair   Something broken; sadness; hopelessness; time to restore something. *What relationship needs repairing?*

report   Being judged; rumours; show up on time; feedback; a sharp noise. *What grade would you give yourself?*

repulsive   Turning away; driven back; something you would rather not look at; a gross scene; a horrible person. *What unpleasant thing is better to let go of?*

rescue   Feeling victimized and needing help; having the right supplies; someone in dire straits. *Who are you trying to rescue?*

resort Time to get away for a while; needing a rest; turning to someone for help. *What's your last resort?*

restaurant Nourishment that someone else provides; eating too many meals in restaurants; needing more choice in your life; choose your nurturance. *How can you give yourself more choices?*

reunion Getting together with old acquaintances; reconnecting with a part of yourself; childhood memories; seeing old friends. *Who do you need to reconnect with?*

revenge Feeling resentful, victimized or wronged; stuck in retribution; a quarrel. *Who are you wanting to get back at?*

revolution A complete change in lifestyle and priorities; an enlightening experience. *Who is ready for a turnabout?*

revolver Being hurt from afar; violence at arm's length; wanting to shoot someone. *Who is moving in circles?*

reward Being paid; needing recognition; thanks for a kind act. *Who deserves a reward?*

ribbon A sign of giving up; surrender; passivity; decoration; getting a reward; recognition for courageous acts; torn into bits; a little girl's hair bow. *Who deserves a medal?*

ride Going along for the ride; not having any choice in direction; letting something ride; ride it out. *Who is being taken for a ride?*

rifle Shooting from the shoulder; going through someone's things; a sharp shooter. *Who is trying to take something from you?*

ring   Repeating patterns; you've been here before; symbol of union or accomplishment; a mystical symbol of wholeness; being a ring leader; having a ring side seat; catching the brass ring; phoning; engagement. *Who do you expect to call?*

rink   Things going smoothly; skating on thin ice; winter sport; hockey. *Who is skating circles around you?*

riot   Out of control; wild colours; without constraint. *Who's making all the ruckus?*

river   Going with the flow; smooth sailing; easy path ahead; a change in lifestyle or job; things are moving fast.   *How could you drop the oars and easily go downstream?*

road   Prescribed path; knowing where you are going; easy-going; taking a fork in the road; look where you're going and where you've been; someone going on the road. (see **rode**)   *What road have you recently started on?*

robber   Trying to get away with something; robbing her; fear of being robbed. *What part of yourself are you robbing?*

robbery   Having something you value taken from you; feeling violated. *Who is committing highway robbery?*

robot   Doing what you are told; being on automatic; unfeeling; mechanical. *Who in your life is acting like a robot?*

rock   Solid, predictable, long term; sometimes a symbol of the inner self; the soul; something on the rocks; being shaken up; moving back and forth; hitting rock bottom; a rock hound; rigid and stubborn; unmoving. *Who do you know you can count on?*

rocket   Flying high; reaching for the moon; having difficulty keeping your feet on the ground; sex; terrific thrust. *What rocket of desire have you recently launched?*

rod   A fishing buddy; stiff and unbending; a man's name; a staff; time for some recreation. *What are you fishing for?*

rode   A trip taken; having come a long way; a horse rider. (see **road**) *Who has recently ridden off into the sunset?*

role   Identification; tasks; the way others see you; going in circles; acting career. (see **roll**) *Who is tired of the role they are playing?*

roll   Tumbling over and over; a barrel; a wad of money; someone hogging the bed; concern about weight; wanting an expensive car (Rolls); changing your position on something; a roll in the hay; time to roll up your sleeves; a roll top desk; being called. (see **role**) *Who is on a roll?*

roller   Moving slowly; going steadily forward; returning cycles; repeating cycles. *What is nicely rolling along for you?*

roller coaster   Ups and downs; the highs and lows of emotion; out of control; cheap thrills. *Who are you on a crazy ride with?*

roller skates   Memories of childhood; moving under your own steam. *What key do you hang around your neck now?*

rolling stones   Lack of stability/commitment; desire for adventure; burning the candle at both ends; insecurity; ongoing musical group. *Who is the rolling stone in your life?*

roof   Something going on in your head; stifling strong emotions; blowing the roof off something; frustration; putting a cap on it; wanting protection. *Who is hitting the roof?*

room   Needing more space and privacy; making room for someone, or a new project. *How are you making room for yourself?*

roots   Firmly planted; stability; ancestry and tradition in the family; getting to the heart of a matter; putting down roots. *What new project is beginning to take root?*

rope   Needing to connect with another; strongly tied to a secure base; getting to know the ropes. *Who is at the end of their rope?*

rose   Love; friendship; intimacy; caring; blossoming; beauty; standing up for something you believe in; looking through rose- coloured glasses.; a girl or woman's name. *Who has risen to the occasion?*

round   Softness; femininity; going around in circles; wholeness. *What has sharp edges that need rounding off?*

ruby   Symbol of love and ancestry; something very precious; symbol of your inner self; longings from your soul; inheritance may be indicated. *Who is the Ruby in your life?*

rug   Feeling flat; walked on; taken advantage of; treated poorly; covering up what's down there. *Who is walking all over you?*

run   Feeling stressed, overworked; hurried; fear; run across someone; running someone down; run for it; run out; feeling run down; something is beginning to feel run- of-the-mill. *Who is running in the dream and how is that dream character like you?*

rust Inexperienced; doing something you haven't done for a long time; sitting around; not getting enough exercise; a colour. *Where are you getting rusty?*

"A dream is a manifestation.
Just like what you live is a manifestation,
but a dream is quicker and easier to achieve,
and not so troublesome
if there's something you don't want."

Abraham-Hicks

Intent upon the truth's unfolding
light and shadow twined in truth
illusion's meaning — self-imploding
we are what your dreams deduce

March 4, 1994

Ruth Cunningham

S

red flowering wounds
my heart's own hot surgery
the healing of dreams
Nora Leonard

sack   Let go at work; needing new clothes; left empty-handed; a container; feeling plundered. *What goodies are in your Santa sack?*

sacred   Spiritual dream; a special message; pay close attention and write, paint, or draw the experience; reflect on it;   a   church, synagogue, or old temple often represents the inner self, the eternal soul. *What do you hold sacred?*

sacrifice   Martyrdom; feeling victimized; having to give up one thing to get another; an energy drain; losing something; a symbolic offering. *Who is making too great a sacrifice?*

sad   Time to cheer someone (yourself?) up; putting a false smile on; needing more sunshine; losing a friend. *What are you sad about?*

saddle   Being in control of where you are going; in tune with your instincts; getting ready to leave for a faraway place. *Who is ready to get back to work?*

safe   Needless worry or fussing; ungrounded fear; a need to keep something safe; putting something in a safe, being protected. *How is being worried about safety interfering with new opportunities?*

safety pin   Joining something; time for some hemming, a quick solution. *What are you pinning your safety on?*

sail   Traveling over emotional currents; going with the flow; shopping; beginning a journey; sailing into someone harshly; feeling tossed around. (see **sale**) *How are you feeling discouraged?*

sailboat   Smooth sailing; peaceful; quiet and gliding; sporty; holiday feeling; wanting to get away from it all. *Who is at the helm?*

sailor Desire to have adventure; envy of others who have exciting adventures; worries about security; eat your spinach.   *Who would rather be sailing?*

saint   Dream of the sacred; having to be perfect; acting better than thou; a mystery may be afoot; a devil in disguise; someone putting up with too much. *Who is acting like, or pretending to be, a saint?*

Saint Bernard   Needing rescuing; out in the cold; a big friendly person. *Who needs to see a friendly face?*

salad   Getting everything mixed up;   eating your greens; remembering youthful experiences. *What is the raw truth you need to look at?*

sale   Feeling as if you are selling a part of yourself; addicted to shopping; someone trying to sell you a bill of goods. (see **sail**) *What isn't for sale?*

salmon Getting back to your origins; a struggle upstream; feeling useless after having children; a message to eat more fish; a symbol for courage and wisdom**.** *Where are you struggling the current?*

salt   Essential; vital substance; survival; tasty; a fisherman; taking something with a grain of salt; someone worth one's salt; time to salt something away; preserving something; a symbol of friendship and hospitality; money worries. *Who is your best friend?*

sand Not on firm ground; time quickly running out; relax and play with your kids in a sandbox; needing more sleep; making things smooth; rubbing off the rough edges; a visit to the desert. *What are you trying to bury?*

sandwich Caught betwixt and between; feeling the squeeze from both sides; too close for comfort; not having any privacy; a quick and easy lunch. *How are you feeling sandwiched in?*

Santa Claus Desire to return to childhood; someone who brings you presents; jolly; comes once a year; needing to be present; someone who laughs a lot. *What are you not giving to yourself or allowing yourself to have?*

sap Vital substance; tree blood; springtime; may indicate health concern; a silly person; becoming sweet. *How is your strength being drained in order to meet someone else's needs?*

sapphire Riches; precious and spiritual stone; money indicated; associated with protection by the Archangel Michael; the jewel of heaven. *What blue-eyed person lights the stars in your eyes?*

sari Covered up with beauty; eastern influence; plenty of cloth; being wrapped up. *What garment are you trying to hide in?*

satellite Circling around someone else's world; flying out of orbit; following. *What message are you sending out?*

saucer Part of a set; underneath the main dish; a saucy person; a shallow dish. *What do you think about flying saucers?*

sauna Things steaming up; cold water will only heat things up; time to relax. *Who is getting hot under the collar?*

saviour   Sacred figure; special representation of your inner self; willingness to do service for others; saving others. (see **sacred**) *Where can you turn for help?*

saw   Cutting through things; using the right tools; dry as sawdust; listening to a wise saying; getting enough sleep. *What have you seen lately that made an impression on you?*

scab Natural healing; protection; taking someone's place; picking away where it hurts. *What part of you is getting better naturally?*

scale Measuring up; competition/comparison; a hard outer layer; a dentist visit; tipping scales; practicing music; climbing high; the sign of Libra; balanced. *How might you rate yourself on a scale of one to ten?*

scanner   Copying someone; spending time at the computer; glancing over things quickly and perhaps missing important details. *What do you need to look at more carefully?*

scar   Leaving a lasting mark; making an impression; an identifying mark. *What scar is long overdue for healing?*

scarecrow A person with straw for brains; someone just flapping in the wind; scared of black birds. *Who are you trying to scare away?*

scarf   Covering up your thoughts; identifying which club you belong to; protecting your neck; unnecessary trimming; gulping something down. *Who do you know who wears a special scarf?*

schedule A need to make plans; keeping track of things; never following your own schedule; hating schedules. *What forthcoming event needs to be scheduled in?*

school Something new to learn about a situation; never too old to learn; early memories; association with competition and measuring up to others' standards; wanting approval from an authority figure. *Whose approval are you seeking and how does that remind you of when you were a student?*

scientist Cold and cut off from one's feelings; logical; making assessments; seeking answers. *Who is acting like a mad scientist?*

scissors A cutting remark: a scissor-lock; two sharp blades; dress making; crafts. *What, or who do you need to cut out of your life?*

scooter Youthful freedom; excitement; vacation; adventure; independence and flexibility of movement indicated; moving quickly. *Who needs more independence?*

scope Measuring depth; wondering how deep a person is; being able to see a long distance ahead; ability to see the future, or to see beneath the surface of things. *What is under examination?*

scorpion Stinging remarks; sexual excitement; deep reflection; treachery; desert; deadly. *Who do you know who has the sun, moon or a planet in Scorpio?*

scratch Just below the surface; someone's claws out; working from scratch; pulling out of a race; having trouble getting it together; lottery win. *What do you need to do to get up to scratch?*

scream Frustration; fright; a need to be heard; anger; making a loud noise. *What are you screaming to say?*

screen Covering something up; not wanting to be seen; keeping something out; going to the movies; needing to be examined; sifting things through; hiding something. *What are you screening out?*

screw   Feeling victimized; taken advantage of; unappreciated; things tightening around you; health problems; being guarded; someone having a screw loose; putting the pressure on; needing to screw up your courage to do something; afraid you might screw up; sexuality. *Who is getting screwed?*

script   Stuck in the same old story; reruns; playing your part; a style of writing. *What script have you become locked into?*

scuba   Getting in beyond your depth; needing help breathing; safely diving into the unconscious, or your emotions; seeing underneath. adapting to another realm. *When are you going to take the plunge?*

sculpture   To shape out; design and build; carving out your future; appreciating beauty; forming beauty from raw materials; working with your hands. *What are you sculpting out for yourself?*

sea Something important for you to see; the letter C might be significant; feeling confused and at sea; beginning a voyage; the source of life; taking a trip. (see **ocean & see**) *What do you need to look at again?*

seal   Closing something off; needing your mark of special approval; closing up the cracks; signed and settled; a vulnerable part of yourself; an adept swimmer. *What secret seal have you broken?*

search   Seeking spiritual understanding; looking for the right mate; needy. *What are you searching for?*

seat Sitting pretty; having a special place; time to stop running. *Where have you seated yourself?*

second   Not first; feeling inferior; not original; at the last second; second gear; seconding a motion: entering a second childhood; feeling like a second-class citizen; having second sight; getting your second wind; seconding a proposal. *What is second nature to you?*

secret   Feeling ashamed and embarrassed; closed off from friends and family; burdened; a secret society; a mystery. *What special secret are you now ready to share?*

seduction   Feeling compelled to do something against your better judgment; a charismatic person you find hard to resist. *How are you being seduced?*

see   View again; looking after someone; seeing your way clear to do something; seeing someone off; see it through to the end; you can see through the subterfuge; religious reference. (see **sea** & **ocean**) *What are you not seeing?*

seed   Beginning of something; unlimited potential; newness; something left to go to seed. *What is just beginning that may grow beyond your wildest dreams?*

see-saw   Difficulty making up your mind; going up and down; playing childish games. *What needs to be balanced out?*

self   Your inner self; other parts of yourself; time to help yourself. *What did the dream self do that was familiar?*

sell   Getting rid of something; betraying someone; selling yourself short; feeling trapped in a cell; selling a part of you off.. (see **cell**) *What new idea are you sure will sell?*

senior   Wise and experienced; having more knowledge; senior high school; older. *What senior has had an influence in your life?*

separate   Feeling pulled apart; keeping yourself away from others; a need to get away; alone too much.   *Who needs to have some space alone?*

sermon   Being told what to do; serious teachings; call that man "sir"; something to learn, or think about.   *When did you last attend a place of worship?*

servant   Serving others; being ordered around; being humble and obedient; felling hard done by. *Who do you wish to serve?*

serve   Your turn; waiting on someone; being helpful; someone gets what serves them right. *How can you better serve yourself?*

service   Caring for someone; working hard for the love of it; the armed services. *Who are you serving and why?*

seven Lucky number; spiritual number representing God in Hindu and Christian tradition; Neptune; music; Seven Wonders of the world; seven days in a week; Seven Deadly Sins; seven dwarfs.   *What significance does the number seven have for you?*

sew   So what; putting things together; traditionally woman's work; needing stitches; a happy note. *What can you do now to save time and aggravation later?*

sewer   Underground; unable to see the light at the end of the tunnel; feeling down and out; getting rid of waste, or waist.   *Who does a lot of sewing?*

sex   Sexuality; love and intimacy; wanting to be physically or emotionally close to another;   high sexual needs; confusion about sexual role. *What part of your sexuality have you been repressing?*

shade Not getting enough sunlight; cool; darkness; fancy sunglasses; protection from hot sun. *Whose shadow are you under?*

shadow Jungian idea of positive or negative aspects of your personality that you resist accepting; Peter Pan association; a shadow of one's old self; under the shadow of someone; the Shadow knows; a shadowy figure; a way to tell time. *What parts of yourself are you unwilling or not ready to accept?*

shake Nervous; quivering; greeting someone new; saying no to something; time to shake the dust off; being shaken up; a swindle. *Who, or what, at has recently shaken your world?*

Shaman Inner self; a powerful and specially gifted person; capable of magic; part of yourself that can magically achieve all that you desire; spiritually advanced; very special figure that you could write about, paint, or draw. *What message did the Shaman have?*

shame Feeling embarrassed and ashamed; regretful about some past deed. *What are you ready to let go of?*

shampoo Washing thoughts; cleaning up; taking care of yourself and your things. *Who needs to clean-up their attitude?*

shamrock Check if that diamond ring is real; a lucky clover. *Who do you know who is Irish?*

shark A predator; greedy; competition and shrewdness; feeling pursued and victimized by a powerful person; fear of the ocean. *Who is the card-shark?*

sharp A cutting or biting remark; clever and witty; changing direction suddenly; quick; being aware of things; attractive to look at; a sharp shooter. *What do you have to keep a sharp eye out for?*

shave   Baring your face; a close shave; something right in your face. *What are you getting dangerously close to?*

shawl   A new baby on the way; keeping warm; a cover up. *Who do you know who wears a shawl?*

shed   A change in personality; a place where you have been keeping and storing parts of yourself for later use; shedding blood. *What old, limiting beliefs are you ready to shed?*

sheep   Following the crowd; passivity; easy prey for wolves; innocence and sweetness; a black sheep turns up. *Where have you been feeling a little sheepish?*

shelf   Shelving an idea; putting something away; organizing. *What did you put on the shelf that should now be looked at again?*

shell   Protection; guarded; hiding from others; withdrawing from the world; being under bombardment; time to shell out; feeling shell-shocked; shell-proof; a symbol of introspection. *When will you be ready to come out of your shell?*

shelter   Protection; taking refuge; hiding out; buying a new home; feeling insecure; overly concerned with survival issues; a tax shelter. *Who are you sheltering?*

shepherd A mystical and spiritual figure; leaving the flock; leadership abilities indicated; self-reliance; the Good Shepherd. *Who are you looking after?*

shield   Guarding; protection; a badge; a large geological piece of Canada. *What part of yourself are you shielding?*

shingle starting a new business; protection; feeling irritation. *What are you itching to do?*

ship   Ocean voyage; adventure; way; waiting for your ship to come in; shipping something. *What is ship-shape?*

shirt   Covering up; getting overly excited; a shirt-sleeve affair. *Who has lost their shirt over something?*

shoe   Feet on the ground; having a solid foundation; message from your inner soul; trying to fill another's shoes; the shoe is on the other foot; scaring something away; operating on a shoe string; a shoo-in. *Who needs to try walking a mile in their adversary's shoes?*

shoot   Hitting the target; reaching a goal; aiming high and hitting the bull's-eye; shooting for the moon; moving quickly; someone growing very fast; shooting stars. *Who is shooting off their mouth?*

shop Something for sale; selling your talents and skills; independence; having your own business; setting up shop; talking shop with associates; window shopping.   *What have you bought recently?*

shopping   Looking for something special; shopping around for something else in your life. *What are you looking for that you don't already have?*

shore   A safe landing; the border; keeping things to yourself; integrating deep parts of yourself; on the edge; reaching a safe haven; holding something up. *What new shores have you reached?*

shot   Someone taking a potshot at you; having a go at it; a shot in the dark; taking pictures; it might be a long shot; all used up and worn out. *What has happened that gave you a shot in the arm?*

shoulder   Overburdened; may indicate health problems; over-estimating your strength; put your shoulder to the wheel; working side by side; tell it straight from the shoulder; giving someone a cold shoulder. *Who could share your responsibilities and help shoulder the burden for a time?*

shovel   Cleaning out old emotional baggage; working hard, snow shoveling. *What do you need to shovel out of your life?*

shower   Cleansing; relaxation through water; ideas falling on you; receiving or giving gifts; a quick rain; being showered upon. *What new ideas do you get while in the shower?*

shrink   Feeling small; psychiatrist; pulling back in fear; needing to talk to someone; half your size. *What problem needs shrinking?*

shut   Closing the door on something; shutting out; shutting off; shutting up; shutting down; a shut-in; a shut-out; time to get more shuteye. *Who are you shutting out of your life?*

sick   Health problems may be indicated; worried about health; focusing on physical concerns; anxiety; fed up with something; sick at heart; sick humour, or a sick joke; feeling attacked; a gross person. *How might the sick one in your dream get well?*

sidewalk   Walking by the side of someone; a street you know well; walking, rather than driving; independence.   *Who's side are you taking?*

sign   Paying attention to details; signing papers; talking in signs or gestures; looking for signs of life; writing your name on a document; a sign of the zodiac; signing up for new employment; sign in and be present; sign off and leave; don't sign everything over. *Who is looking for a sign before they act?*

silhouette   Seeing the outline only; no substance; mystery; in sharp relief. *Who does the silhouette in the dream remind you of?*

silk   Riches; wealth indicated; exploring sensuality; relationship to the Orient and the exotic; jumping with a parachute; a jockey's colours. *Whose skin is as smooth as silk?*

silver   Concerns about aging; looking into a mirror; eloquent speech; purity; connected with the moon; money issues; a twenty-fifth anniversary; the cloud with the silver lining; wanting to be in the movies; the family silver. *Who is getting silver in their hair?*

sin   Feeling guilty or wronged; acting self-righteous; violating a religious belief; missing the mark; fear of the devil. *What "shoulds" are you ready to let go of?*

singing   Happiness and joy; wanting to tell the world about your success; feeling one's soul lift; spilling the beans. *Who is singing their little heart out?*

sink   Time to move up and out; a sinking feeling in your stomach; sink that basket and score; washing; everything but the kitchen sink; going deep within; a clogged drain; fear;   disappointment, or dread. *What might be giving you that old sinking feeling?*

sister   Soul self; supporting;   a woman close to you or similar; a woman for whom you have sisterly feelings; competition; affection; closeness; a part of yourself that you see in your sister; religious order; a nurse; feeling connected to women.   *Who do you feel competitive with and close to at the same time?*

sit   Stationary; having trouble sitting still; commanding; restriction; waiting for something to happen. *Who needs to get some exercise?*

six Six sides; in numerology, it represents happiness, accomplishment, joy; very positive number; a teacher; the symbol of the I Ching; a unifying number; 666 is the Biblical number of the beast (Satan) but considered good luck and most favourable in China; a six-shooter; having a sixth sense. *How is the number six relevant in your life?*

skate Moving quickly across a smooth surface; ability to balance; challenge and accomplishment; a type of fishing; moving on wheels; bored with where you are going. *Who is skating on thin ice?*

skeleton Essentials; the bare bones of an issue; getting to the center of things; the long term; underlying issues; fright; may indicate possible health concern related to bones; a long, thin person; a framework; Hallowe'en. *Who is rattling the skeletons in your closet?*

ski Balance; moving with speed and ease; a love of winter; it's all downhill now; moving smoothly across country. *How can you stay focused as you move quickly and easily through this challenge?*

skin Sensuality and intimacy; sexuality; may indicate health concern over skin problems; largest organ of the body; facing the outside world; appearance; saving your skin; a skinflint; in a superficial manner; watch out for a skin game; between the outer and the inner; protection; an animal skin is a symbol of power; got through by the skin or your teeth. *Who is thick skinned?*

skirt Femininity; freedom of movement; sexuality; dancing; skirting an issue. *Who do you know who chases skirts?*

skull May indicate health concerns related to head; headaches; sinus difficulties or allergies; ancestry and what you have inherited; rowing the boat all by yourself; a poisonous relationship; feeling pirated; inner thoughts. *What bare bones facts are in front of you?*

sky   Reaching for the upper limits of your potential; getting a larger perspective on your problem; able to see things coming from a distance; air element; being grounded as you reach for the sky; something that comes out of a clear blue sky. *What ideas are you eager to bring into the world?*

slap   Insulted; doing things in a slap-bang or slap-dash manner; slap-happy; a short, powerful swing; knocking yourself out to make people laugh. *What have you just slapped together?*

slavery   Being taken advantage of; not liking what you do for a living; being plagued inside with have to, should, and must; living with a slave-driver. *How do you feel like a slave?*

slide   Easy departure; things sliding; going downhill; time to play with some kids; reaching home safely; water slide.   *Who is letting things slide?*

slip   Losing your balance; not watching where you are going; being careless and moving too quickly; protection; an underlying issue; moving smoothly or secretly; escape quietly; letting something slip; slip up and make an error; giving someone the slip; start new growth from an old plant or source; something slipshod. *Who, or what,is throwing you off balance?*

slope   Going downhill; easy movement; slight decline or incline in your feelings; losing control; skiing or sledding. *Which way are you going on the slope?*

slow   A need to slow down; paying attention to details; subtleties; replaying past events; moving in slow motion; behind the times; a slow poke; someone with dark eyes. *What part of your life do you need to replay in slow motion to better see what happened?*

smell Something stinks; sticking your nose in where it doesn't belong; nosing around; acute memory. *What message from the past is this smell bringing to you?*

smoke Difficulty breathing; letting your anger build up; making peace; health concern related to lungs and sinuses may be indicated; fire somewhere; smoking out something. an addiction. *Who is putting up a smokescreen?*

smother Feeling smothered; not having your own space; needing more air. *What are you covering up?*

snail Slow-moving; wanting to go more quickly; living in a shell; carrying all your worldly goods on your back; small and vulnerable. *What is moving at a snail's pace?*

snake Transformation; letting go of old patterns; shedding your skin; fear of change; sneaky; spiritual symbol; dangerous; biting remarks; medical symbol for healing; a snake in the grass; special change and message indicated. *Where in your life are you tempted?*

snob Feeling inferior; low self esteem; having to prove something; thinking you are better than others. *Who do you think is better than you and what about that bothers you?*

snow A cold or frozen part in you; cover up; not able to move forward easily; feeling snowed under; watching too much TV; pure and white; a unique individual; snowmen are cold. *Who is getting snowed?*

soap Cleansing; removing toxins; the aftermath of swearing; a slippery road ahead; someone on their soapbox. *Who is hooked on soap operas?*

soaring   Extremes of emotion, feeling depressed, or elated; forgetful; not paying attention to where you are going; hurting other people's feelings; being angry. *Where are you sore?*

soccer   Part of the team; not allowed to touch with your hands; fancy footwork. *Who is quick on their feet?*

sock   Protection; hitting someone; warmth and safety indicated; wind sock. *Who would you like to sock?*

soda Bubbly and happy; drinking too much sugar; someone is crackers over soda; a soda jerk. *Who is hooked on sodas?*

soldiers   Protection;   authority figures; doing what you are told; obeying orders; acting without thinking for yourself; conformity; ants or aunts around; taking on responsibility; look out for the soldier of fortune. *Who is being the good little soldier, looking for a medal?*

sole   Getting to the bottom of things; taking a walk; reference to soul; feeling alone; eternal life; special message from your spiritual inner centre. *What sounds fishy?*

son   Youthful; energetic; idealistic; masculine side; heroic; impulsive; protecting; defending; a son or someone who is like a son. (see **sun**) *What message is your young, masculine part giving you?*

song   Happy; making a big song and dance over something; time to celebrate; a psalm. *What did you get or give away for a song?*

soup   Afraid of getting involved in something you may not be able to get out of easily; fond memories of childhood; difficulty moving around; urban angst; beefing up your energy. *Who has recently found themselves "in the soup"?*

south   Below; a young man going south; wanting a warmer climate. *Who's the left-handed one?*

spacecraft   Wanting to get away fast; feeling overwhelmed; desire to escape from mundane responsibilities; wanting adventure; moving fast; not having enough of your own space; feeling spacey; a trip to inner space. *Where are you crafting a new space for yourself?*

spank   Fed up with your kids; having a spanking good time; feeling guilty about something. *Who would you like to spank?*

sparrow   Small but not insignificant; going to the birds; feeling small and intimidated. *What is your little dream bird telling you?*

spear   Good aim; feeling victimized; pinned down; primitive violence; a pierced heart. *What are you aiming for?*

spectator   Just watching; not taking part; afraid to get involved; an avid sports fan. *What do you need to jump into?*

speech   Needing to say something; someone who talks too much; a course in public speaking. *What is the speech you wish you'd made?*

spelling   Spelled out clearly; casting a spell; feeling under a spell; doing your duty; filling in for someone; taking a rest; a spelling bee. *Who would you like to spell you?*

spending   A love of shopping; financial worry; overextending yourself; an emotional deficit; feeling spent; a spendthrift. *What do you spend your time on?*

sphere   Wholeness and perfection; surroundings; planets; heavenly bodies; Earth. *What sphere of influence is surrounding you?*

spider   Spiritual symbol of mother; natural instincts; devouring mother may be indicated; creativity; spending too much time on the world wide web. *What kind of web are you weaving for yourself?*

spill   Flowing; careless; taking a fall; don't cry over spilled anything; overflowing. *Who spilled the beans?*

spin   Spiral; time going by; missing out on something;   too many worries about wasting time; going in circles; taking a long time to tell it. *What's the hurry?*

spiral   Feminine spiritual symbol; cycles of death and rebirth; creative thought process; snail or sea shells; constantly increasing or decreasing. *What are you spiraling toward?*

spirit   High spirits; alcoholic drinks; phantoms; may indicate communication with someone has passed on and who has a message for you; feeling good; enthusiastic. *What is the special message that this higher power has for you?*

sponge   Soaking it all up; a special cake; someone sponging off another. *Who is ready to throw in the sponge?*

spoon   A nice cuddle in bed; born with a silver spoon in their mouth; eating soup; confusing one's words (spoonerism). *Who is being spoon fed?*

sport   Competition; trying as hard as you can; team spirit; making fun of someone; have a sporting chance; a sporty person. *Who is not being a good sport?*

spring   A jumping-off point; beginning; spring is in the air; new growth; love and romance; change and release from old ties;

something has sprung a leak; a spring chicken – or not; having spring fever. *Who is wound up as tight as a spring?*

square   Symbol of wholeness; the four elements of earth, air, water and fire; the four directions, east, south, north and west; being logical and as straight as an arrow; a square deal; being square with someone; needing to square up; square dancing; having a square meal. *Who is being a square?*

squirrel   Running madly around; storing up for the winter; a fertility symbol in Japan; able to leap fearlessly, trusting that support will be there. *Who is going a little squirrelly?*

stab   Someone turning on you; slander; anger and jealousy; fear; a stab in the dark; taking a chance. *Who is not getting the point?*

stag   A large proud male; going alone to a party; a men-only affair. *Who's the buck?*

stage   Performing; wanting applause; recognition; going through things one step at a time; making plans and carrying them out; stage-struck. *What are you having stage-fright over?*

stairs   A precarious climb up or down; be careful where you walk; pay attention to each step you take; one thing leading to another; moving up in the world. *Who is running up and down the stairs?*

stallion   Male sexual symbol of power, ability and strength; instincts; the power of the body. *Who is the stud?*

stamp   Mailing a letter; putting your mark on something; frustration and impatience; assertive; angry; returning to your old stamping-grounds. *What are you trying to stamp out?*

star   The heavens; a spiritual directional symbol; horoscope; heading for fame; seeing stars; thanking your lucky stars; star-crossed lovers. *What is your wish upon a star?*

statue   Immobility; inability to move forward; frozen and locked in; stillness; on a pedestal. *Who is cold and unyielding?*

stealing   Wanting something that belongs to someone else; feeling sneaky; selfishness; lack of caring for others; stealing away; a really good bargain; stealing someone's heart. *What, or who, are you bracing yourself for?*

steam   Hot, healing and cleansing; reaching a boiling point; pushing hard ahead; running out of steam; letting off steam; steam rolling over people. *Who is getting all steamed up over nothing?*

steep   A precarious position; up too high; a steep price for something; give something a good soaking; a sharp slant. *What are you steeped in at the moment?*

steps   Taking life one step at a time; moving forward; being careful about your next step; caution; keeping in step; someone out of step; taking steps to change things; stepping down; time to step on it; taking baby steps; a step-relative. *Who is stepping up?*

stew   A mix-up; confusion; feeling lost amid the crowd; not standing out; blending in; anxiety and worry; a man named Stu; stewing in your own juices. *Who is in a stew?*

stick   Needing defense; having strong commitment; staying with something or someone because you promised; playing with a hockey stick; shake a stick at; living in the sticks; cheating on someone; wanting to stick around; something sticking out; a stick-up; stick figures; a stick-in-the-mud. *Who walks with a big stick?*

stiff   Health risk may be indicated; muscle tension or joint problems; acting stiff; rigid or inflexible; unwilling to change; stiff-necked; a stiff penalty; a stiff decision; being drunk; a working stiff. *Who is rigid and uptight?*

stomach   Tension; poor eating habits; finding something really hard to take; difficulty in digesting new information. *What are you having trouble stomaching?*

stone   Symbol of the eternal, unchanging inner self; hard and unyielding; a heart of stone; a gravestone; a gem-stone; leaving no stone unturned; out-of-date; stone broke; stone deaf; only a stone's throw away; a stony stare; casting the first stone; Rolling Stones. *What stone is precious to you?*

storm   Possible difficulties; feeling in a muddle with a group of people; strong emotions raging out of control; thoughts or emotions whirling around.   *What relationship in your life would you characterize as stormy?*

stove   A change by fire; hot issue indicated; warmth; memories of mother and family gatherings; feeling sentimental. *What is getting too hot to handle?*

straight   Having a goal and moving toward it; being on the straight and narrow; moving between two forces facing each other; conforming to the norm; time to act straight away.   *How can you be straighter about your feelings with the people around you?*

stranger   Character representing a new part of ourselves; describe the stranger and reflect how this description might fit you; starting something new. *How is your life stranger than fiction?*

strangling   Health concern may be indicated; air supply cut off; feeling overwhelmed; crushed by others' problems; unable to speak. *What do you feel is holding you back?*

strawberries   Possible food allergy; fresh and delicious; summery personality. *Who has strawberry blonde hair?*

stream   Stream-of-consciousness; emotions; a steady flow; going with the current. *What do you need to streamline?*

student   New learning; remembering your school days; a beginner; taking something seriously; inexperienced. *What is important for you to know right now?*

submarine   Feeling enclosed and surrounded; going deep into things; protection. *Who is sinking into deep emotions?*

subway   Moving underground; something changing in your unconscious; taking a new route; a long sandwich; traveling. *What new awareness has opened up for you?*

suffocation   Someone invading your space; not having enough room to breathe; feeling watched or followed around; not enough freedom. *Who is smothering you in the name of love?*

sugar   Being too sweet; saying sweet, empty words; wanting a sugar daddy. *Who is sugar-coating things?*

suicide   Self destruction; Sue sitting by your side; feeling alone and hopeless; a message to talk to someone about your problems. *What part of you do you want to get rid of?*

suitcase   Wanting to escape; packing up; carrying around old resentment; planning a trip. *Where do you want to be?*

summer   Relief, joy and holidays; taking it easy; taking time to enjoy the beauty of nature; time with friends and family; turning somersaults to please someone. *What could you learn by reflecting back to last summer's holidays?*

sun   Reaching up; doing a lot of thinking and analyzing; coming out of darkness; dealing with some very hot issues; new things under the sun for you; put on lots of lotion; getting burned; masculine symbol. (see **son**) *How can you let in more light?*

sunrise   New beginnings; may be referring to son or dawn; hope for the future; stretching and feeling the pleasure of being alive; morning. *What is new under the sun for you?*

sunset   Things settling down; completion; closure; a time to rest; a son set in his ways; evening. *What is setting for you?*

superman   Taking on big responsibilities; trying to do too much at once; placing health at risk; placing burdensome expectations upon yourself; having two opposite identities.   *Who is behaving like a superwoman or superman?*

supermarket   Having lots of choice; nurturing yourself; someone great at marketing; needing to serve yourself; getting treats. *How can you make supermarket shopping more agreeable?*

superstar   Desiring fame; wanting attention; high achievement goals; needing recognition; your dream superstar character has qualities you possess yourself, but are not acknowledging. *How are you similar to the superstar of your dreams?*

surfing   Wanting high thrills; taking risks; riding on the wave of the future; waiting for the big one; leaping when the time is right; feeling free. *Who do you know who surfs?*

surgery   Cutting away a part of yourself; rejecting parts of yourself; health issues may be indicated; changing your body or face to suit another; fear of an operation; looking at life-and- death issues; inner changes; cutting remarks made to you. *Who is about to receive surgery and how do you feel about it?*

swallow   Someone small and bird-like; dainty and timid; taking something in without thinking it through; living in a barn; a message of spring; having to swallow words of anger; feeling overwhelmed and swallowed up. *What are you finding hard to swallow?*

swan   Calm, serene, leader; calm after the storm; family indicated; feelings of sadness; preparing to exit with a swan song; taking a swan dive; the swan is a romantic and ambiguous symbol of light, death, transformation, poetry, beauty and melancholy. *Who do you know who is as graceful – and grumpy – as a swan?*

sweat   Working hard; health issue may be indicated; hormonal shifts; anxiety and overworking the heart;   night sweats; worry, fear and anxiety; breaking out in a cold sweat; enduring; having to sweat something out; working in a sweat shop; passion. *What is causing you to break out in a sweat?*

sweets   Not getting enough protein or satisfying food; lacking the sweetness of life; bitter sweet; being sweet on someone; needing sweetening up; a sweetheart; whispering sweet nothings; someone giving you a lot of sweet talk; having a sweet tooth; a saccharine tongue. *Who is too sweet to be true?*

swimming   Success indicated; taking the plunge; moving through difficult issues with ease and a clear sense of direction; staying on top; being comfortable while moving through emotional situations; getting exercise. *Who is doing just swimmingly?*

swing   Moving back and forth on an issue; indecision; feeling torn between two attractive offers or opportunities; difficult to pin down; a hypnotic person or situation; making things work; in full swing; working the swing shift; remembering swing music; a swinger. *When did you last go high on a swing?*

sword   Accuracy; defense; cutting to the heart of the matter; competition and winning; logic and cold analysis; a guardian of the magic sword of Avalon; capable of justice, fair defense and honour; at sword's point; feeling as if the sword of Damocles is hanging over you. *What old attachments do you need to cut away?*

sympathy   Feeling badly for another person; worry about someone; sadness; agreeing with someone's sad state. *For what part of yourself do you feel sympathy?*

symbols   A sudden loud clanging; everything in your dreams and life is a symbol; a dream dictionary like this one. *What do the symbols in your dream and life tell you?*

symphony   Playing in harmony; making music together in a harmonious team environment; love and romance indicated. *What instrument would you be in a symphony orchestra and why?*

"Reality is merely an illusion,
albeit a very persistent one."
Albert Einstein

$\mathcal{T}$

Body is a cage,
with hinges rusted, askew
it cries to dance.
Shirley Leonard

table   Planning; coming to the table to talk, negotiate; making a decision; getting a group of people together; eating; family gathering; reversing conditions, as in turning the tables; times tables.   *What decision can you put on the back burner for a while?*

tablet   A special message; a pill; time to write a letter; reference to medication. *What will you write on your tablet?*

tag   Identification; knowing how much something is going to cost; marking something for later reference; catching up with someone; following after. *Who are you playing tag with?*

tail   Something behind you, following someone; the end of something; retreating with your tail between your legs; parting remarks, taking a chance on heads or tails; in a tail spin.(see **tale**) *Who is the tattle tale?*

tale   A falsehood; making up stories; your life story. (see **tail**) *Who is telling tales out of school?*

talk   A talkative person; gossip; talking back; talk over something with a friend; someone has something important to tell you; lots of tall talk going around; talk it out; someone talking down to you; the talk of the town; talking shop too much; talk someone through something; time to talk turkey; someone talking through their hat. *Who is talking too much?*

tall   Growing concerns; someone or something getting big; reaching high; something taller than you thought; a tall order. *Who has been telling tall tales?*

tampon   Possible feminine health issue; feeling blocked; repressed sexuality; concerns about menstrual flow; gynecologist visit. *What are three reasons you enjoy being female?*

tango   Fantasies of Latin lovers; sensuous; daring; life may be getting dull. *What have you recently dipped into?*

tank   Strong, powerful force moving forward; mowing down everything in its path; pushy, aggressive; seemingly indestructible; a large container; somebody tanked up; wearing a tank top. *Who is built like a tank?*

tap   Health concern re urinary tract; unable to stop the flow of a powerful energy; a secret code; a leaky faucet; something ready and on tap; time to tap into something; being tapped on the shoulder; a tap-dancer; the bugle call for lights out, time to sleep . . . and dream. *What opportunity is tapping on your door?*

tapestry   A colourful story told in embroidered pictures; a tangle underneath; *Who is weaving a spell around you?*

tar   Feeling black and stuck; someone who has the same faults, as in tarred with the same brush; a sailor. *Who do you feel like tarring and feathering?*

target   Feeling singled out; an easy target; getting your aim straight; knowing your target. *What is your next big target?*

Tarot   Fortune-telling; symbolism; prophetic dream; relying on others to tell you what to do; look within for the answers. *What are you wanting to know?*

tart   A sharp, acid taste; sexual freedom; indulging in sweets; dress flashily or gaudily. *Who is the tart?*

Tarzan   Strong masculine figure; swinging around; natural man who communicates with animals; unafraid; a positive, protective inner masculine figure for woman; an empowering inner figure for a man who desires freedom of expression; need to return to the simpler life. *What part of you is hearing the call of the wild?*

tattoo   Identification; telling the world who you are; making a permanent statement; bucking authority and conformity; wanting to be seen as daring, exciting, rebel, risk-taker; sailors; hearing the beat of your own drum. *What significance is the dream tattoo?*

Taurus in Astrology, the sign of the bull; stubborn; bull-headed; strong; long- lasting; someone born between April 21 and May 21. *Who has been giving you a lot of bull?*

taxi   Someone else at the controls; temporary ride; lack of commitment, pay as you go; fast pace; taking a while to lift off. *When will you be ready to get into the drive's seat?*

tea   Tea for two; tea and sympathy; time for a tea-break; a name that starts with T; herbal tea; drinking too much caffeine; four o'clock tea; golf. *Who are you tee'd off with?*

teapot   Something you are soaked in; let it sit for awhile before you act; social gathering. *Who would you like to invite for tea?*

teacher   Memories of being in school; instruction and tests; measuring up and achievement; rebelliousness; having something to share and teach others; teach somebody a lesson. *Where are you concerned that you are not measuring up?*

tears   Repressed sadness; feeling sorry about something; mourning; regret and loss; not wanting to cry in front of others; loving to go to tear-jerker movie. *How are your dream tears an expression of the sadness that you don't want others to see?*

technology   Keeping up with the latest inventions; needing to upgrade your computer; taking a computer course; feeling bombarded with machines. *Who is acting like an unfeeling robot?*

teeth   A common dream symbol is teeth falling out; could be time to see a dentist; may indicate that you are having difficulties related to self-esteem and speaking your mind; feeling powerless or self conscious; fear of rejection; not being taken seriously; being armed to the teeth;   ready to fight tooth and nail; something that has set your teeth on edge; paying attention to details; chewing away at something. (see **tooth**). *What would you really like to sink your teeth into?*

telephone   Receiving an important message; having to deal with constant interruption; being on call; communication indicated. *Who have you been putting off phoning?*

television   Watching too much television; time to be a star in your life; a vision is telling you something. *What are you escaping from through television?*

temper   Repressed rage; anger and frustration; acting cool when you aren't feeling so; tempered steel. *Who is the hothead?*

temple   A call to worship; sacred issues; a dream temple; thinking; Shirley Temple. *What sacred part of your life have you been ignoring?*

ten   Ten-to-one; Ten Commandments; bowling; being tenth; ten people.(see **number**) *What happened when you were ten years old?*

tennis Playing at love; all dressed in white; a society game; getting a sore elbow; going to court. *What's your racket?*

tent   Going camping; protection from the elements; getting back to nature; an oxygen tent; a wedding tent; portable shelter. *How could you simplify your living conditions?*

terror   Concern over something; extreme fear; repression (see **nightmare**). *What are you afraid will happen?*

test Performance anxiety; worries about failure; feeling unprepared; afraid of being put to the test; a test case; test driving something. *Where are you being tested?*

testament   Saying something very special; the truth for all time; telling others your philosophy; proof. *What in your life is a testament to who you really are?*

textbook   Learning; school; competition; worries about exams; getting good marks; studying either too much or too little; a textbook case; reference. *Who needs to hit the books?*

theater Art; wanting to perform; putting on an act; exaggerating a problem; not being honest about yourself; hiding your true self behind a mask. *What role are you playing?*

thermometer   Measuring; heat rising; feeling nervous, frightened; may indicate health concern related to fever. *What is rising too high or going too low for comfort?*

thief   Someone you cannot trust; as thick as thieves; stealing something. *What has been stolen from you?*

third   Feeling third-class; coming in third; need to get into lower gear; feeling like a third wheel; number symbolizing conflict; concerned about Third World countries (See **three**). *Who's giving you the third degree?*

thirst   Not getting enough water; thirsting for knowledge; dried up. *What do you thirst for?*

thirteen   Still considered bad luck, but originally a lucky number; a founding group; living on the thirteenth floor; feminine number. *What are you superstitious about?*

thorn   Protection; a thorny issue; a chance for someone small to help someone big. *What, or who, is the thorn in your side?*

thread   Hanging by a thread; a delicate link between people; winding in and out; a common theme; sewing. *What obstacle course are you threading your way through?*

threat   Feeling endangered; anxiety and fear may be indicated; worried about someone or something; having something valuable taken away from you. *Who, or what, is a threat to you?*

three   An extra person; feeling awkward with a pair; three is the number of conflict, spirituality and growth; aligning body, mind and spirit; three strikes and you're out; feeling confined in three dimensions; a three-point landing or turn; life feeling like a three-ring circus. (see **third**) *How is three significant to you?*

threshold   At the beginning; on the verge of a change; a revelation. *What is your dream telling you about a new undertaking?*

throat   Speech; self expression; afraid to speak; sing your own song; in a cut-throat business; having something rammed down your throat. *What is stuck in your throat?*

throw   Being tossed aside; getting rid of something; ancestral throw-back; throwing cold water on an idea; throwing good money after bad; throw one's hand in; throw your lot in with others; throwing yourself at someone or into something; sick of something or someone. *Who is throwing their weight around?*

thumb   Thumbing a ride; thumbs up or thumbs down; a thumbnail sketch;   someone who reminds you of Tom Thumb; thumbing one's nose at someone; all thumbs over it; *Whose thumb are you under?*

thunder   Storm coming; possible rain ahead; hearing rumblings; a loud person; excitement; repressed anger; stealing someone's thunder; being thunderstruck. *How might you take advantage of this powerful emotional energy?*

tiara   Wanting to be treated like a queen; feeling special; needing attention. *What can you do to make yourself feel special?*

ticket   Permission to enter; a way to get in; overstaying your time; *What is just the ticket for you?*

tidal wave   Caught up in overpowering emotions; repressing strong feelings; may be a premonition dream; fear of disasters. *What is changing so fast it threatens to overwhelm you?*

tie   *Tied up in knots; a joining or bond; ending in a tie; formal party; getting married; too many activities. Who is fit to be tied?*

tiger   Connection with cats; feeling wild; listen to your instincts; tiger-lily; in Chinese beliefs, tiger is symbol of inner power; trying to change your stripes; a wild man; a hunter. *Who is acting like a tiger?*

tightrope   Delicately balanced; one wrong move and you fall; potential loss of footing; a need to stay present; tension and performance anxiety. *Where in your life do you feel as if you are walking a tightrope?*

time   It's about time; feeling you don't have time to do everything; ahead of your time; remembering the good times and the bad times; losing no time; something too time-consuming; pass the time of day; a time-honoured custom; having the time of your life; needing some time out; Father Time lurking; wasting time; killing time; keeping to a timetable; acting at the right time; timing is everything; serving time; feeling as if you are sitting on a time-bomb; behind the times. *What important thing are you going to do even though you say you have no time?*

tip   Feeling off-centre; getting a hot tip; showing how grateful you are; something on the tip of your tongue; feeling tipsy; on the extreme edge; emptying out contents; something ready to tip the balance; tip your hat; feeling you have to tiptoe around. *What has happened that you know is just the tip of the iceberg?*

Titanic   Tempting the Gods; end of a romance may be indicated; wanting adventure; feeling helpless; going down; out of your depth; something sinking. *Where has the impossible happened?*

toast   Wishing someone well; getting warm and cozy; eating a good breakfast. *Who is toast?*

toboggan   Something sliding out of control; childhood memories; on a slippery slope; winter sports. *Who is rapidly going down hill?*

toe   Health issue may be indicated; inappropriate foot   wear; aggressive, not taking no for an answer; fear of being left out; staying on your toes; having to toe the line.(see **tow**)   *In what are you trying to get a toe-hold?*

toilet   A toxin flush in your body and attitude; letting go of resentments; let them have the toy; control issues. *What are you afraid to let go of?*

tomb   Fear of death; feeling buried alive; enclosed; held back; stopped. *What part of your self have you buried?*

tongue   Speech; wanting to say something; sharp-witted; sensuality and sexuality; seduction; saying something tongue-in-cheek; someone needing a tongue lashing; the cat's got your tongue; tongue-tied; hanging your tongue out for someone or something. *Who is having trouble keeping a civil tongue in their head?*

tooth   Continuing in spite of opposition, paying attention to details; a sore tooth; believing in magic. (see **teeth**)   *When did you last see or feel a fairy around?*

tornado   Emotions in a whirlwind; feeling buffeted by strong emotions; unpredictable; a part of nature; an energetic kid; a industrious homemaker. *Who is the tornado?*

torture   Feeling tortured, either by your conscience or your circumstances; someone punishing you; pain in the body; someone else in control; not wanting to scream out your pain.   *How are you torturing yourself?*

toupee   A cover up; vanity; a hairy situation; secretive; to pay for something. (see **rug**) *Who are the two you have to pay?*

tourist   Travel; getting away; a foreign part of yourself; feeling like a tourist in your own town; not going first-class; visiting other people's lives. *When were you last a tourist?*

tow   Needing help; being pulled; a light-haired person. (see **toe**) *What are you dragging behind you?*

towel   Mopping up the mess; drying out; dry up; laundry day. *Where are you tempted to throw in the towel?*

tower   Thinking tall thoughts; leaning one way; a change in life circumstances; leadership; standing tall and strong; inflexible; determined; something towering over you. *Who is your tower of strength?*

town   Time for entertainment; on the town; painting the town red; someone living in a town-house; a memory of simpler living. *What are you ready to go to town on?*

toy   Playtime; enjoyment with children; feeling like someone is discounting you, putting you down, or minimizing you; treated like an infant; grown up toys. *Who is toying with your emotions?*

track   Stopped in your tracks; running after something; off the track; on the wrong side; making a track record; you are on the right track. *What, or who, have you lost track of?*

traffic   Going in circles; stress; feeling stuck; watching signs carefully; dealing with something illegal; communication. *Where are you going along with public opinion?*

tragedy   Deep sadness; remembering a misfortune or an accident; mourning; over dramatizing. *How is your dream showing you another way to look at tragedy?*

trail   Falling behind the pack; marked path with turns, twists and surprises; nature walks; being a trail-blazer. *How are you leaving markers along the way so you can find your way back?*

train   Taking a course; travel; being on track; following the prescribed route; going along with what everyone else is doing; a long bridal veil or skirt; taking the fast train; in training; wanting a free ride; taking the e-train; riding the subway; a toy train; letting off steam; racing through intersections; blowing your horn. *What are you in training for?*

trampoline   The ups and downs of life; feeling elated; freedom from gravity for a few seconds; joy; taking pleasure in physical sensations; freedom of movement; athletics indicated; taking a tumble; a soft landing. *What exercise program have you started?*

transit   Taking a journey; public transit may mean going along with what other people think or do ; conformity; transitory; check what planets are transiting your astrology chart now. *Where are you going?*

transparent   Seeing through a disguise or a facade; consider what you are not looking at; open and frank; something becoming clear. *Who is being transparent but thinks they are fooling others?*

trap   Feeling you have to do something that you don't want to; setting a trap; feeling betrayed; unable to move. *Where are you feeling trapped?*

trash   A part of your life you are finished with; looking down on others; a time to clean up; letting go. *What are you trashing?*

travel   On the go; feelings of anticipation; a holiday; lack of commitment; a temporary stay; new horizons opening up. *Where are you planning to go?*

treasure   A special part of yourself; talent; discovering something valuable; relief from poverty; prosperity indicated; a loved one. *What do you treasure most in yourself?*

treat   *Giving yourself a small luxury; not giving yourself enough pleasures; you may be ignoring and suppressing your desires for something better; ice cream time. What, or who, needs a treat?*

tree   Symbol of history, life, and fertility; protection from a harsh environment; taking a firm stand; dependable; being sure and solid about where and who you are; as plentiful as growing on trees; Tree of Knowledge; not seeing the forest for the trees, or vice-versa; feeling up a tree. *What can you learn from your family tree?*

tree house   Desire for natural living; childhood memories; wanting to get away; stuck-up. *What did you learn or experience in your dream tree house?*

trial   Being judged; feeling defensive; wrongly accused; trial-and-error; taking a trial run; being tested. *Where are you being tried?*

triangle   Three-sided object symbolizing power moving to the top; special spiritual symbol, such as Maiden, Mother, Crone, or Father, Son, Holy Ghost; any trinity; conflict; three's a crowd; visionary; a call to dinner; childhood music. *Who is caught in a love triangle?*

trick   Not knowing what to expect; someone putting you down; at a disadvantage; expecting one thing and getting another; you don't miss a trick; knowing the tricks of the trade; trick-or-treat. *Who is up to their old tricks?*

Trinity   Spiritual symbol; often appears to Christian dreamers; symbolizes the creative aspect, bringing a concept, idea or vision into the world; a sign for the spiritual seeker.(see **triangle**) *Where is three significant?*

trip   Time for a holiday; nervous about a forthcoming trip; someone coming to visit; watch your step; time to trip the light fantastic; trip up someone; on a bad trip. *If you could go anywhere in the world, where would you go, and why?*

triplet   Three similar issues or people; good things come in threes; body, mind, spirit connection; let the trip happen; three in a row. *What three people have said similar things to you?*

trophy   A victory; a prize well-won; something on display; an ego-booster; taken as a remembrance; recognition; a hunter. *What possession is your biggest trophy?*

trouble   Feeling ganged- up on; taking the trouble to do something for someone; finding a trouble-spot; being a troubleshooter; getting yourself into trouble. *Who's the trouble-maker?*

truck   Moving; feeling burdened; driving a truck; keep on trucking; a long-distance driver. *What load have you been carrying?*

*****trumpet*****   *A call to listen; a call to action; proclaiming loudly; a hard-of-hearing person. What are you not saying that needs to be said loud and clear?*

trunk   Carrying emotional baggage around; not letting go of old hurts and resentments; old memories; an elephant trunk could be masculine sexuality; main part of your body; men's trunks; car trunk. *What baggage is your dream telling you to let go of?*

trust   Could indicate difficulties with self-trust; fear and inability to act; taking something on trust; something to do with a trust fund; having confidence. *What are you not trusting yourself to do?*

truth   Telling the truth; being honest and straightforward with people in your life; trying to fool yourself, or others; a lie detector test. *What have you been lying to yourself about?*

t-shirt   Youthful appearance; feeling free, unencumbered; liberated; casual; getting a message across. *What message do you want on your t-shirt?*

tub   Cleansing; relaxing; nurturing yourself; a beauty bath; an old boat; a tubby person. *What needs to be washed away?*

tune   Listening to a tune; a desire to write music; being in sync; using your intuition; in tune with your feelings; time to change your tune; can't get that tune out of your mind; feeling out of tune; Looney Tunes. *What, or who, do you want to be more in tune with?*

tunnel   Birthing symbol; going through a difficult passage; coming out the other side to freedom and joy; darkness before the light; feeling squeezed and tense; seeing light at the end of the tunnel; pushing your way through; going underground. *Who has tunnel vision?*

turkey   Thanksgiving or Christmas; time to talk turkey; someone gobbling everything up; the country Turkey; going cold turkey. *Who needs to settle down to business?*

turn   Taking your turn; not knowing which way to turn; turning away from something; turn the other cheek; turn a deaf ear; turn down a proposal; turn a person's head; turn an honest penny; time to turn in; turn in one's grave; being turned- off; a turn-on; time to turn over a new leaf; turning the tables; turn turtle and run; a turncoat about to appear; it's your turn now; a turning-point; a good turnout; a quick turnover; getting stuck on the turnpike; going through a turnstile. *Who, or what, is turning you inside-out?*

turquoise   Semi-precious stone; symbolizes healing and spirituality to the Aboriginal people; sacred stone of the Navajo, associated with natural forces and healing; the colour of the sea. *What part of you needs the healing power of the turquoise?*

turtle   Sticking your neck out; moving slowly but steadily; a symbol for the Earth; having a hard shell to hide in; yummy chocolates; a turtle-neck sweater; helpless on your back; a race for survival. *Who is your turtle- dove?*

twelve   Dirty dozen; cheaper by the dozen; a big omelet; a number signifying completion; wholeness; spiritual number; twelve disciples; twelve days of Christmas; twelve hours in a day or night; Twelve Tribes of Israel; twelve months. *What does twelve mean in your life?*

twenty   An age of change; moving out of adolescence and preparing for adulthood; two tens, which represent transition, making twenty a doubly significant number; seeing your life from a completely different perspective. *What were you doing at twenty that's similar to what is going on in your life now?*

twilight   Something coming to an end; feelings of nostalgia; moving toward the finish of a project; softer perspective; mellow; romantic; interest in the twilight zone; partial narcosis, as in twilight sleep. *What in your life is approaching its twilight time?*

twin   A part of you, possibly opposite to the way you normally see yourself; two who are alike; ideas and decisions; coming in twos; in Astrology, Gemini; joining up with someone; seeing double. *Who would you like to twin up with?*

twist   Feeling bent out of shape; needing to visit a chiropractor; yoga; distorting someone's words; snack food; a wild dance; Elvis. *Who is trying to twist you around their little finger?*

two   Going to somewhere; having too much; a couple; putting two and two together; a two-bit person; two can play at that game; a two-edged sword; a two-timer; worth two-bits; a twosome. *Who is being two-faced?*

typewriter   Living in the past; an old reporter or writer; a writer of a certain type; needing to write something down; a resistance to computers; a limited memory. *When did you last use a typewriter?*

tyrant   A bossy person; being told what to do; having a lot of should's coming from your inner voice; feeling pushed and forced to do something; being hard on yourself; judgmental. *How are you being tyrannical with yourself?*

"Dream images are sketched in fugitive ink,
and if we don't re-experience them immediately,
they fade to invisibility on the fast turning pages
of waking consciousness.
Jill Mellick

U

patient inner work
sorting the scraps
piercing a soul quilt
Nora Leonard

udder   Something needing to be released; a need to utter something; mother's milk; nourishment. *What feels like a chore?*

UFO   Something foreign in your life or body; acting in a strange manner; throwing plates around, unable to identify something that is flying around you. *What part of you are you having trouble identifying?*

ugly   A rejected part of yourself trying to get your attention; paying too much attention to surface issues; look deeper; feeling like an ugly duckling; not realizing your potential for beauty or talent. *Where is your swan hiding?*

ukulele   Hawaiian holiday; relax; making happy music; just strumming. *Who is stringing you along?*

ulcer   Repressed anger; burning issue. *What's eating you?*

umbilical   Dependency; being joined; a pregnancy; time to cut the apron strings. *What do you need to break away from?*

umbrella   Turn it over and catch the pennies from heaven; rain; a sun umbrella; a parent company; a broader perspective. *What do you need protection from?*

umpire   Playing catch up; calling the play; foul ball; someone watching your every move; hiding behind a mask; well protected. *Who is judging your hits and misses?*

unable   Trying too hard; feeling limited; trying to do too much all at once. *How are you underestimating or overestimating your abilities?*

unaware   Not paying attention; something important about to happen which may surprise you. *What could you look at more carefully?*

unbalanced   Needing to bring balance to your work and/or home life; extremist attitudes; time to get centered.   *What do you need to balance things out?*

unborn   New ideas forming; something not ready yet; a time of preparation; potential. *What are you getting ready for?*

uncle   Having had enough; someone who reminds you of an uncle. *Who's twisting your arm and trying to make you do something you don't want to do?*

uncooperative   Not getting what you need; an antagonistic person; being too nice all the time.   *What part of yourself are you not cooperating with?*

under   Feeling down; looking underneath the surface; under the weather; under age; speaking under your breath; going under cover; something right under your nose; getting under way;   feeling under a cloud; Australia. *What is hanging over you?*

underground   Something going on under the surface; a change in lifestyle may be indicated; something being ground under; knowing a secret way to get out; British subway.   *What have you buried under there that needs to come to the light?*

underwear Feeling exposed; taking care of details. *What is your true identity underneath all that outer appearance?*

undress Removing your identity; taking off the mask; showing your true self. *Who do you want to be?*

unemployed Working too hard; afraid of losing your job; not working hard enough; not doing what you want to do. *Who do you know who is unemployed?*

uneven Not balanced; feeling that things are not fair; an odd person; not smooth sailing. *How are you feeling cheated?*

unfaithful Feeling deceived; losing your faith in something or someone; making promises you can't keep. *How can you be more faithful to yourself?*

unicorn Magical instincts; phallic symbol; belief in the impossible; something with unusual medicinal properties. *What special place would you like to visit?*

unicycle Doing it alone; going around in circles; one wheel; a balance act. *Where are you peddling alone?*

uniform Not enough variety in your life; needing a change; you are not your clothes; identity; a cover up. *Who wears a uniform, or when did you wear one?*

unintelligible Having difficulty making yourself understood; something not clear; a mystery. *What do you need to know?*

union Wanting to be attached to something or someone; belonging to a group who protect your interests; loyal to your country. (see **marriage**) *What do you need to feel complete?*

unisex   Unsure of your sexual orientation; knowing we are all one; feeling one sided; wanting to be the other sex. *Who dresses in unisex clothes and hair styles?*

universe   A BIG dream; wanting the whole thing; feeling expanded; being in touch with the source. *What is at the centre of your universe?*

university   Higher learning; more to learn; challenges; memories of university; feeling better than others; high achiever. *Who needs to learn what?*

unload   Time to get rid of excess baggage in your life; take a load off your feet; rest; talk to someone; keeping a heavy secret. (see **unpack**) *What do you need to let go of?*

unmask   Time to remove your mask; covering up doesn't work anymore; your true identity coming out; knowing the truth; a masquerade party. *What have you recently found out?*

unpack   The holiday is over; time to get organized; sort out the stuff you've brought back; moving day. (see **unload**) *What do you need to unpack that you have been holding on to?*

unplug   Too much energy around; disconnecting; letting your emotions flow; being plugged in. *What do you need to detach from?*

unprepared   Performance anxiety; feeling you don't know enough; avoidance; doing too much; unsafe sex. *What haven't you prepared for and why?*

unprotected   Needing protection; unsafe sex; feeling vulnerable; a young scared part of yourself. *Who, or what, needs protection?*

unselfish   Doing too much for others; needing to look after your self more; being the martyr. *Who needs to look at their motives?*

unthankful Resentful; given something you don't want; forced to feel grateful. *What do you want that you would be thankful for?*

untidy   Rebelling; too busy; not looking after yourself; not being in the moment. *What do you need to take care of?*

up   Thumbs up; giving more thought to your actions; thinking before you speak; mind; an optimistic person: the jig is up; up and at 'em; up against something; on the up and up; time to get up; something is up and coming; up in arms over something; having ups and downs; up to date. *What's up with you?*

uphill   A struggle to get somewhere; moving in the right direction. *What does your dream tell you that will make the climb easier?*

upper   Being above it all; keeping a stiff upper lip; upper class; upper bunk. *Who has the upper hand?*

upset Losing your balance; a disturbance; something been overturned; a queasy stomach. *What is being turned upside-down?*

urgent   Doing too much; rushing around; someone about to give you an important message. *How are you acting hastily, when slowing down might give you a more balanced approach?*

urine   Release of pent up emotions; health issues to look at; signal to wake up and go to the bathroom. *Who are you pissed off with?*

urn   Thinking of a person who has passed on; a social function with lots of tea or coffee; a special urn. *What have you earned?*

useful   Giving or needing help; feeling inferior; invention; making oneself useful. *What is useful about your dream that will help you in waking life?*

usher   Someone guiding you to your place; showing you the way; going to the movies or theatre; a wedding coming up. *What new place or situation are you being ushered into?*

uterus   A place of growth and new birth; a warm safe place; being aware of one's safety;   mother matters; someone pregnant; expecting something new. *What is germinating in you?*

utopia   Ideal life; or situation; wanting perfection; living on a beautiful island. *What changes does the dream Utopia suggest?*

utter   Time to speak up; complete and total. (see **udder**) *What is it you want to say or write?*

U-turn   Something left behind; going too fast in one direction; time for you to turn; changing your mind quickly; illegal action. *What did you forget to mention?*

"It is the effort required to remember dreams
and the resulting stretching of consciousness
that finally opens up dream reality."
Jane Roberts (Seth)

$\mathcal{V}$

icy snow, head lamps
awe inspiring mountains
slip sliding away
Amy Palmer

vacant   Feeling empty; no thought; lack of caring and honesty; an empty place; new spaces opening up; someone showing no interest; a vacant lot. *What changes have you been through lately that have left an empty feeling within you?*

vacation   Time to get away and take a rest. *What did you do on your last vacation that you are still thinking about?*

vaccinate   Needing protection; getting ready for a long trip; afraid some bug will get you. *Who is needling you?*

vacuum   Someone draining you of energy, open space; an opportunity for you to move into; sucking up; taking your lunch to work. *What vacuum is ready to be filled?*

vagabond   Feeling a need to wander; too many responsibilities; time to declutter. *What do you want to run away from?*

vagina   Womanhood; a special entrance; an exciting journey; fear of pregnancy. *What embarrasses you most about being a woman?*

vagrant   Fear of loss of financial security; being an outsider to your social group. *Who is loss and wandering around?*

valentine   A secret admirer; romance in the air; a message about the heart; Valentine's day; wanting love. *Do you have, or are you, a secret admirer?*

valley Down in the dumps; looking up; getting a different perspective; a dip in the relationship; needing to take the downs with the ups; feeling enclosed. *Where could you rest awhile?*

valuable   Important item;   getting the most value for something; feeling worthless. *What precious thing is your dream showing you?*

vampire   Unsatisfied sex drive; late night; overindulgence threatening to overwhelm you; have your blood checked; life may be too dull. *Who or what is draining you of your life energy?*

van   A person named Van; carrying too much stuff; a move may be coming up. (see **car**) *Who do you know who owns a van?*

vanilla   A flavourful life; baking; something losing its flavour; white. *Who prefers vanilla to chocolate?*

varnish   A shiny cover up; glossing it over; someone with a hard outer coat; for external display only; only for show; needing protection. *Who is acting in a superficial manner?*

vase   Flowers given or received; a container.   *What feelings are you holding in?*

Vaseline   A need for protection; dry skin; vulnerability. *Who is being slippery?*

vault   Spending money too quickly; saving money and valuables; jumping too quickly; high arches; storing things. *How can you vault over the obstacle in your life?*

vegetable   Slang for not being smart; energy source; vegetarian; vitamin; sun energy. *Who has raw energy to spare?*

vegetarian Concern for health; needing more energy; feeling pressured to eat right; sensitive to animals. *Who do you know who is a vegetarian?*

vehicle Traveling; carrying something; something to take you wherever you want to go. (see **car**, **van**, **train**, etc.) *How do you get to where you want to go?*

veil   Hiding; a bride; hiding tears; curiosity about the beyond; a nun; misty. *What are you hiding?*

vein   Taking something to heart; being in a certain mood; the road by which you nourish yourself. *Where is your vein of gold?*

Velcro   Feeling stuck; easy to open; being noisily ripped apart; a temporary sticking; easily stuck. *What are you having trouble tearing yourself away from?*

velvet   A hidden iron fist; wealthy; smooth; rich; soft; cozy. *Who has a velvet voice?*

vending machine Small change; mechanical buying; frustration, junk food; a quick bite. *What are you buying or selling without thinking too much about it?*

ventriloquist   A dummy in the picture; close lipped; doing the speaking for others; the real source of the information; holding a dummy on your lap; having lots to say. *Who are you talking for?*

verse   Experienced; skilled; regular stress; a special way with words. *What verse in the Bible or literature is most helpful to you now?*

vertebra   Backbone; able to stand up to it, segments; you are as young or as old as your back. *Who is not getting enough exercise?*

vertical   Straight up and down; standing up to be counted; something needs to be straightened up. *What is up (or down) there for you?*

vest   Showing your arms; furnish with power; authority; take possession of; having a vested interest in something. *What is the third piece to the set?*

vet   Love and care of animals; something to be checked out; veteran; a war vet. *In what field have you had a lot experience?*

viaduct   a bridge; high over something; by way of a duck. *What heavy traffic are you carrying right now?*

vice   Clenching a jaw; holding on tightly; undesirable habit. *In what part of your life do you feel squeezed?*

vice-president   Second in charge; proud of your vice; number two. *Where are you feeling like the second in power?*

victim   Feeling helpless; fear; not knowing how strong you are; having had enough; time for change. *Who or what has made you not believe in your own power?*

video   Recurring images; old tapes playing; time to change the pictures; missing the big picture. *What story are you playing over and over again?*

village   Small town thoughts; country living; a sense of belonging; knowing all your neighbours. *Where is your ideal village?*

villain   Less-than-virtuous thoughts; a need to protect yourself. *Who is the villain in your drama?*

vine   Creeping; wending its way; tenacious; climbing the walls; higher education. *What is slowly attaching itself to you?*

vinegar   The sweetness of life gone sour; a sour-faced person; drying up. *Who is in a pickle?*

vineyard   Ancient plant; a hot country; a sphere of activity; spiritual work; sour grapes; Italy. *What would you like to celebrate?*

violence   Undue force; breaking a law; fear of losing control; someone not facing what is troubling them; seeing too many tv shows or movies. *Who is using excess physical force to make a point?*

violet   Shy; retiring; sweet smelling; the colour of violets; a female name; Africa. *Who do you know who is a delicate violet?*

violin   Sweet music;   high pitched; strings too tight; being serenaded; music of the gods. *What beau is making overtures?*

virgin   Pure, fresh, new; unspoiled; inexperienced; someone named Mary; someone born in Virgo. *What new venture are you undertaking?*

visit   Forthcoming visit; time to call a friend; punishment. *What is it that you have to revisit and have a better look at?*

visitor   Something or someone on their way; unexpected company. *Who is expecting a little visitor?*

vitamin   Needing more energy; check your supplements; nutrients. *Who needs better nourishment?*

voice   Needing to speak up; a message from yourself; being in good voice; voicing your opinions; finding your unique voice; self expression. *What did your dream voice say to you?*

volcano   Time to let the steam out; pressure building; a violent outburst; new land forming; Hawaii. *What is about to erupt?*

volleyball   Remembering school days; tossing the ball back; a need for aerobic exercise; part of a team. *Who is volleying stuff at you?*

volunteer   Being roped in for something you don't want to do; helping out. *What are you sorry you said you would do?*

vomit   A need to get rid of something; disgusted; an upset stomach. *What is turning your stomach?*

voyage   A lengthy journey; a new undertaking; probing space. *Where would you like to go?*

vulture   A large bird of prey; fear of death; cleaning up what nobody else wants; someone ready to pounce when you are weak. *What can you do to gain more strength?*

"Dreams call from the imagination
to the imagination and can be answered
only by the imagination."
James Hillman

W

from a mythic source
flutter iridescent dreams
bent on becoming
Nora Leonard

waffle   Undecided; talking on and on; eating a good breakfast; home cooking. *What are you having trouble deciding?*

wagon   Childhood memories; on or off the wagon; really happy about something. *Which star have you hitched your wagon to?*

waist   Not making the best use of something; a halfway point; caught in the middle. (see **waste**) *Who is waist high?*

wait   Not time yet; concerned about weight; staying up for someone; acting like a servant. (see **weight**) *What are you waiting for?*

waiter or waitress   Eating out; serving and care-taking for someone; waiting. *Who is acting like a servant?*

walk   Time to slow down; get more exercise; use a wok for cooking; getting away; walking a thin line; on strike; a walkabout; reconsider your walk of life; time to walk away; walking on air; walking your talk. (see **wok**) *Who is walking all over you?*

wall   Feeling closed in; feelings blocked off; rejection; sadness; loneliness; barrier to get through; keeping something out or in; feeling as if you are climbing the walls; driving someone up the wall; some off-the-wall idea; building walls or tearing them down; afraid that some walls have ears. *Who has their back to the wall?*

wallet   Questioning your identity or wanting a change; financial difficulties; buying too much on credit; overspending.   *What's in your wallet?*

wallpaper   Cover up; not standing out enough to get the attention you need; blending in so well you become invisible; new decorations. *What are covering up?*

walnut   Good furniture; eating more nuts; a nutty person who bangs on your wall. *Whose picture do you have on your wall?*

waltz   A romantic evening; old fashioned; the past; something of Walt's; 1. . . 2 . . . 3—go. *Who is dancing as fast as they can?*

wand   Strong intuition; hot, fiery feelings; something pointed out; hoping or waiting for something magical to happen. *If you had three wishes, what would they be?*

war   Suppressed rage; conflicting feelings; unresolved problem; an expensive conflict; remembering a war; afraid of war-clouds; giving the war cry; experiencing a war of nerves; a war pension; a war widow; a war zone; a need for excitement.   *How is what your wore in your dream significant?*

warehouse   Homelessness (Where is my house?); insecurity; loss; unable to find where you belong; a new life experience; wanting a new home; looking for your true home; a new business. *What do you have in storage?*

wardrobe   Identity; how you view yourself; adventures with a lion and a witch; time to recycle some clothes. *What new clothes might better express your new, and emerging identity?*

warm   Warming up to something; being given warmed up leftovers; feeling embarrassed; cozy and safe; cuddly. *What situation makes you feel overly warm?*

warrior   Fighting mad; protecting others; defending your honour; using your strength. *Who is afraid they won't measure up?*

wash   Needing to clean something up; changing the way you talk to people; feelings of failure; time to begin fresh; all washed up; something now colourless; washed away; something that will come out in the wash; a wash-and-wear type of person; washing your dirty linen in public; washing your hands of a situation; expected to believe something that won't wash; a wishy-washy person. *What needs a good cleaning?*

wasp   Bad-tempered;   spiteful; making nasty comments; needing to stand up for yourself; feeling safe and secure; feeling stung by another's comments;   White Anglo Saxon Protestant issue. *What irritating or pesky thoughts are flying around you now?*

waste   Not using something appropriately; grief over things not accomplished; wasting your breath over a situation; waste not, want not; wasting words. (see **waist**) *Who is wasting their life?*

waste basket   Time to clean up; concern over your waist; wasting something; wasting your breath; wasting words; wasting away. *What do you need to get rid of?*

watch   Warning; paying attention; under pressure; time running out; feeling pressed for time; being watchful; taking your turn on duty; watching your step; being watched; in a watch tower; a special watch someone gave you; little reward for long labour. (see **time**) *What time constraints are worrying you?*

water   Deep feelings of love; events happening beneath the surface; look in unlikely places for the answers; water is a central and significant symbol in dreams symbolizing emotion or the unconscious: water behind a dam—emotions being bottled up; stagnant water—emotional life stale or unhealthy; running water—lively emotions, deep water—deep emotions; check if you are drinking enough water; casting your bread upon the water; something watered down; making your mouth water; a waterbed;   Water Closet (toilet); meeting at the water hole; needing softening; water sport; water under the bridge; watercolours; a waterway; feeling waterlogged; a watery grave. *How is the water in your dream like your emotions in your waking life?*

watermelon   Summer memories; sloppy eating; juicy; sweet. *When was the last time you enjoyed having watermelon juice dribble down your chin?*

wave   Repeating action; waving goodbye; riding the wave; on someone else's wavelength; on a wave of success; letting go of a claim; a heat wave; making waves; wave it aside, it's not important. *What is relentlessly coming back to you?*

wax   Getting bigger; pregnancy; a hard veneer; a candle; something melting away; a need to soften up; a protective coating; being wax in a person's hands; wax paper; waxworks; encaustic painting. *What, or who, are you protecting and why?*

weak   Afraid to take a stance; a weak link; a belief there is a weaker sex; feeling weak-kneed; having a weak moment; finding their weak spot. *What's coming up for you next week?*

wealth   Money worries; powerful; feelings of inferiority;   fear of poverty; there is enough for everyone; deserving more. *How much do you need to feel prosperous?*

weapon   Armed and ready; defending or attacking; feeling vulnerable. *Why do you need a weapon?*

web   Hooked on the Internet; deception; preparing a trap; feeling trapped; a web-footed creature; the web of life. *Who, in the whole wide world, would you like to talk to?*

wedding   A joining; romance; a waking life wedding; spiritual considerations; a union; celebration; remembering a wedding. *What part of yourself do you need to know more intimately?*

weed   Addictions; boredom; a need to express wildness; something overgrown; it will grow anywhere; a widow, or widower's, weeds; a nuisance; tenacious. *What needs to be weeded out?*

weight   Having waited long enough; loaded down; concern over your's or someone else's weight; heavy thoughts. (see **wait**) *Who isn't pulling their weight?*

welding   A joining under heat; made into one form; parents; grandparents; relationships; a strong bond; needing eye protection. *What needs to be brought together with fire?*

well   Feeling great; health issues; something deep down that needs to be brought up; leaving well enough alone; a well adjusted person; well behaved; well born; well beloved; well chosen; well built; well connected; well done; well dressed; well endowed; well established; well fed; well heeled; well kept; well liked; well made; well mannered; well matched; well organized; well paid; well prepared; well read; well rounded; well spoken; well thought of; well used; well worth it; well,well,well. *Who has been dredging stuff up from the past?*

west   Traveling west; Mae West; western hemisphere; getting away from it all; aboriginal wisdom tells us west is the direction of strength and introspection; the west coast. *What is in the west for you?*

wet   Training for a new position;   drink plenty of water; a lack of enthusiasm about something; time for a change; someone being a wet blanket; having an erotic dream; nurturing others as a wet-nurse. *Who is a little wet behind the ears?*

whale   Having a whale of a time; a really big issue; loud crying; whale citing. *Who is making a big splash?*

wharf   Ready to take a dive off the deep end; time to unload your burden. *Who is waiting for their boat to come in?*

wheat   Bread and baked goods; breakfast time; prosperity and a change for the better; food allergies. *What is ready to be harvested?*

wheel   Going round and round; fulfillment; completion; taking hold of the controls; coming full circle;   wheeling and dealing; wheel of fortune; a cog; wheels within wheels; wheelies; a big wheel; going in circles. *Who needs to take the wheel?*

wheelbarrow   Pushing or pulling a big load; yard work. *What big wheel is pushing you around?*

wheelchair   Lack of control; needing assistance; hating to stay put; feeling stuck. *Who is struggling to do too much alone?*

whip   A painful situation; moving too fast; unable to defend; punishment; cool whip; turning around very quickly; whip-up; whiplash; a whipping post. *Whois ready to give up?*

whirlpool   Going around in circles emotionally; getting pulled or sucked into something; having fun in a swimming pool. *What situation do you feel helpless to get out of?*

whirlwind   Fast-paced; hectic; a blowhard; tornado; blown away. *What is changing your direction?*

whiskers   Covering up; hiding an identity; giving thought; a pet cat; knowing if you can get through or not. *Who does he remind you of?*

whisper   Inner messages; speaking quietly; telling yourself something that you are having trouble listening to; soft spoken; afraid of the truth; fearful. *Who is the gossip?*

whistle   Time's up; getting caught red handed; attention-grabbing; as clean as a whistle; blowing the whistle on someone or something; wet your whistle; whistling in the dark; living in a whistle stop; a whistling kettle. *What is demanding your attention?*

white   Purity; innocence;   blindness; hot; difficult to define; a hot issue;   covering something up; wanting to white out something; something being whitewashed; bleeding someone white; processed goods, as in white bread, white flour, white sugar; a white-collar worker; someone who wears a white coat; a white feather – symbol of cowardice; a white-elephant; surrendering; white-knuckle fear; a little white lie; a white tie affair; white water adventure; a white wedding. *Who has frozen their feelings?*

whore   Not valuing yourself; selling yourself cheap; a type of frost; shame; sexuality. *How are you selling yourself short?*

wick   Burning up; center of things; passivity;   waiting; the need to shed some light on it; annoyance; working your way down to something. *What are you feeling stuck in the middle of?*

widow(er)   Feeling abandoned; loneliness; a second chance; losing a valued part of yourself. *Who is afraid of being alone?*

wife   The better half; a new role; commitment; fish wife; help meet; feeling trapped; marriage. *Who does the dream wife remind you of?*

wig   Cover up; acting insincere; illness; hair loss; acting another part. *Who is concerned about losing their attractiveness, or their power?*

wild   Angry; ready to attack; instincts running wild; illegal strike; sowing wild-oats; holding a wild card; authors Oscar Wilde or Stuart Wilde; the wild west; acting crazy. *Who is wild and reckless?*

willow   Putting down roots; Wind in the Willows; bending with the circumstances; weeping; feeling droopy; lithe and slender; easy to grow; a blue Chinese pattern on plates; long and slender; delicate. *What, or who, does the willow remind you of?*

wimp   Resignation, feeling less than; unfounded fear; hidden anger; feeling ashamed for not speaking up; angry at someone for not defending her or himself. *What are you afraid will happen?*

win   A lottery win; fear of losing; being victorious; win over someone; win the day; feeling that you can't win; needing to be a winner in order to be accepted; a person named Win. *What are you competing for and why?*

wind   Unpredictable; unseen strength;   change; going around and around; something beginning to wind down; not getting enough exercise; passing wind; getting your second wind; getting wind of something; figuring out which way the wind blows before acting; off like the wind; having the wind taken out of your sails; throwing caution to the wind; a wind instrument; wind power; a windfall;

feeling tense and all wound up; winding someone around your little finger. *Who is the wind bag?*

windmill   Returning to basics; going Dutch; needing more energy; going round and round; alternate energy; tilting at windmills. *What natural energy can you rely on?*

window   Looking out, or in; being watchful; the eyes are the window of the soul and so are your dreams; hiding behind a facade; something transparent; working on your computer too much; something no longer useful and out the window; window shopping. *What window of opportunity has opened up?*

wine   In mythology – the nectar of the gods; a change in spiritual direction; something to be transformed; experiencing an altered state of awareness; feeling sorry for yourself; a religious experience; a dinner date. *Who is the whiner, or wino?*

wing   Escape or wanting to get away; restriction of freedom; acting flighty; staying behind the scenes waiting for your cue; someone under another's wing; a desire to fly away; on the wing; stretching your wings; flying; an plane trip. *Who needs a wing and a prayer?*

wink   Keeping a secret; flirting; a hint or a warning; a need to take forty winks; doing it in a wink; briefly seeing half the picture. *Who is the big tease?*

winter   Being stuck; cold or indifferent; time to cool down over an issue; something needs to rest for a while; cozy down; someone being unfriendly; time to hibernate and rest; winter sport; winter holiday. *How can you bring more warmth and sunshine into your life?*

wire   Feeling wired and tense; walking a thin line; expecting a message; a wiry person; getting your wires crossed; being wire tapped. *Who do you need to contact?*

wisdom   Learning new things; being patient; taking all sides into consideration before making a decision; reflecting on the past; someone looking up to you; a wisdom tooth; an old wise friend; a special book. *Who, or what, do you look for your wisdom?*

wish   Wishes coming true; a wishing well or fountain; making a wish a reality; make a wish and say it three times. *What if you really got what you wished for?*

wisteria Climbing up the social ladder; a good time to make important connections in your community; smelling nice; a spring day; wistful. *Who is the desperate housewife?*

witch   Magic; a nasty woman; old knowledge; the witching hour; having secret knowledge; which is which; dressed in black. *What is magical and unconventional in your life?*

witness   Afraid of getting involved; being objective; getting a perspective on the situation; watching your thoughts. *How are you observing life and not fully participating in it?*

wizard   Powerful skill or insight; an old man with wisdom; magic in your life. *What magic do you want from the wizard?*

wok   Eat fresh vegetables; going for a walk; eastern philosophy; feeling as if there is a fire underneath you. (see **walk**) *How might the Orient provide some answers?*

wolf   Hungry; family loyalty; community; mate for life; time to howl; eating too fast; being the hypocrite; something wild and natural that is howling to come out; feeling overly protective; perhaps crying out for help too often; afraid of the big, bad wolf; struggling to keep the wolf from the door; a wolf in sheep's clothing; wolf whistles; feeling as if you have been thrown to the wolves. *Who is going it alone?*

woman   Nature; mother; feminine values; liberation; woe to man. *Who is the special, wise woman in your life?*

woman friend Someone you love, admire and envy; confident; exactly like you, or exactly your opposite. *How does this woman help you to form your identity?*

womb   Safe; protected; holding something precious; warm and comfy; a cramped space. *Where can you hide out for a while?*

wood   A heavy sleeper; out of danger; natural materials; wooden and unfeeling; memories of a woodshed; woodwind instruments; someone who works with wood; would. *Who "would if they could"?*

woodpecker   Noise-maker; persistence; communication; not being heard; beating your head against something hard; opportunity knocking. *Who is trying to get your attention?*

wool   Cozy and warm; sheep; being shorn; daydreaming or wooly thinking; a knitter. *Who is trying to put the wool over your eyes?*

word   Important message; a promise; a warning; taking back what you said; having the final say; coming to the point; being brief; speaking for someone else; keeping your word; a person of few words; difficulty speaking; word of mouth; a word processor; a word to the wise. *When do you not pay attention to what people are saying?*

work   Feeling valued; getting something done; following through on a commitment; in the planning stages; getting rid of something quickly; the whole thing; getting all worked up; out of work; not working at what you like to do; working your fingers to the bone; stuck in the Protestant Work Ethic; a need to work out something; working wonders; a workaholic. *Who is working too hard?*

world   Big thoughts; a holistic approach; success; in high spirits; something wonderful; going on forever; feeling worlds apart; getting the best of both worlds; thinking about the next world; plans that are out of this world; wanting to travel and see the world; world weary; worldly wise. *Where in the world would you like to go?*

worm   Feeling lowly; down-to-earth; crawling around; wriggling out of trouble, or into it; another dimension; having a worm's eye view; fish bait; a cur. *Who is surviving even though a part has been cut away?*

worn   Working too hard; getting too close for comfort; a warning; tired and weary; Warren; used up. *Who is all worn out?*

worry   Time to change your thoughts; a need to take action; being too passive; time to claim your own power; write out the worst that could happen and let it go; knowing worry never solves anything. *Who is the chronic worrier?*

worship   Looking for guidance; feeling vulnerable and weak; going to a higher source; prayer. *Who, or what, do you believe in?*

worth   Wondering about your worth; lack of confidence; feelings of inferiority; time to value yourself and your talents; you deserve the best; deciding what something is worth. *What can you start doing that will improve the quality of your life?*

wound   Healing; hurt feelings; not paying attention; a war wound. *What old wound do you need to let go of?*

wrap   Completion; protection ;   taking the blame; a gift; keeping something under wraps; taking the wraps off; feeling all wrapped up in something. (see **rap**) *What, or who, is all wrapped up?*

wreath   Moving in circles; something twisted around; in mourning; Christmas; a funeral. *What has encircled you?*

wreck   Feeling wasted; salvaging a ship wreck; a car wreck; somebody always seems to ruin it; a rec centre. *What was wrecked and what did you learn from it?*

wrench   A heartbreak; rejection; a good twist; moving slowly; being pulled apart; a mechanic. *What old hurt are you having trouble letting go of?*

wrestle   Struggling with a difficult issue; conscience might be bothering you; a wrestling team; TV sport; feeling held down; restrained. *What issue are you wrestling with now?*

wring   Being in a tight squeeze; frustration; a need to relax; feeling forced to do something; through the wringer; ringing your hands. (see **ring**) *How can you be more assertive in stating your needs?*

wrinkle   Possible problem brewing with a new project; conflict that needs to be resolved before proceeding; concern over aging; new much sun; smile lines; character lines. *How are you working toward aging creatively and bringing your life-purpose to fruition?*

wrist   Flexibility; wrist watch; bracelets; handcuffs; keeping an eye on time. *Who do you feel has tied your hands?*

write   Receiving an important letter or message; feeling right about something; cancel something by writing it off; write down your dreams; a writer; paying attention to the writing on the wall. (see **right**) *Who do you want to write to?*

wrong   Having the wrong idea about something; time to re think an issue; needing to be right all the time; afraid of getting on the wrong side of someone; feeling someone can do no wrong; on the wrong side of the tracks; get started on the wrong foot; feeling wronged.   *Who do you need to forgive?*

"Wiser and more humorous than we,
dreams remind us that we are subject
to larger forces and influences
than we tend to acknowledge
on a daily basis."
Jill Mellick

X

all hope gone he feels,
desperate, he climbs the tree,
his body hangs—empty
Alberta Nye

X Afraid of making a mistake; Malcolm X; site of buried treasure; X marks the spot; signifies a name for one who can't write; a secret brand in a taste test; memories of an exhibition; adults only; x-rated; a kiss; a vote. Roman Numeral 10; X for the initial chi of Gk Khristos, Christ; plotting a graph. *What did you learn from the last mistake?*

Xena A strong woman with her own identity; battling enemies; saving people; a good friend; someone who was a bully changed into a defender. *Who is the Amazon woman in your life?*

Xerox Boredom; repetition; feeling out of control; copying someone or something. *What issue needs to be enlarged, or shrunk, for you to have a clearer perspective on it?*

X Files A mystery; spooky; suspense; a cover up; visitors from alien places. *What is the mystery you are wanting to understand?*

Xmas A short Christmas; in a hurry. (see **Christmas**) *What is your favourite Christmas and why?*

X-ray Health issues; feeling under scrutiny; focusing on the surface of an issue. *Where do you need to look beneath the surface?*

xylophone Making music; all that jazz; Caribbean holiday; music that gets into your body; pounding away. *Where can you go to be happy and carefree for a while?*

We have traveled on the darkness
wind across the starlit space
swept ahead of heart's confusions
sent within your mind's embrace

March 4 , 1994

Ruth Cunningham

γ

deep in the shadows
I hear my heart pound as if
coming to a crossroads
Nora Leonard

yacht   Ready for a holiday; luxury; wanting to sail away; a yacht club. (see **sale** and **sail**) *Who is cruisin' for a bruisin'?*

yak   Talking a lot; working hard; feeling like a beast of burden. *Who is fed up with idle chatter?*

yam   Getting to the root of the problem; wild yam; maturing woman; sweet potatoes. *What is buried within you that is now ready to be harvested and enjoyed?*

yard   Paying attention to your own business; being nosey and intrusive; making headway; you're three feet away; having a lawn sale. *What is right in front of you that you are neglecting?*

yarn   Lies; telling stories to get out of something; playful antics; arts and crafts; a person who knits. *Who has been spinning yarns?*

yeast   Feeling tired; low energy; food allergy may be indicated; something rising to the surface. *What is brewing beneath the surface?*

yell   Needing attention; your inner self wanting to get a message to you. *Who is not hearing you?*

yellow Yellow fruit; yellow clothes; caution light; the sun; an artist; baby chicks, egg yolk. *What are you afraid of?*

yoga   A new twist; exercise and meditation. *How is this dream experience speaking to your spiritual growth?*

yogurt   Relationship going sour; rage; difficulties digesting milk products; fermentation; interest in health. *Who is the sour puss?*

yoke   Feeling entrapped; unfairly judged; a need to break free; joined to someone; a burden. (see **yolk**) *Who has you on a collar?*

yolk   Nutritious food; a new beginning has been cracked; high cholesterol; a yellow centre; eggs benedict. (see **yoke**) *What is hard boiled?*

young   Reminder of the past; feeling inexperienced and/or inferior; patterns formed in childhood. *What unresolved issues from your childhood is your dream pointing to?*

youth   A new beginning; new job; new relationship; inexperienced. *Who is the youth in your life and what is their message?*

yo-yo   Up and down; childlike fun and challenge; playful. *Who has you on a string?*

"The magic mirror
of the dream does not lie."
Jeremy Taylor

Z

twilight communion
walking between sun and moon
pondering my dreams
Nora Leonard

zebra Someone in jail; Africa; a zoo visit; feeling as if you live in a zoo; street crossing in Britain; wearing stripes. *Who sees only the black and white in issues?*

zero Emptiness; anything is possible; a need to zero in on something; at the beginning or end of something; zero-hour approaching; holding a space; ground zero. *What is adding up to a big fat zero?*

zigzag Taking the long way; feeling confined; sewing; rick rack trim. *Where are you going this way and that?*

zip Racing around; keeping your mouth zipped, check the postal code; compacting information. *What are you in a hurry to do?*

zipper Finishing a relationship or job; closing something up; being careful about what you say; talking too much, a Zip Code. *What are you finished with?*

zodiac Being overly dependent on what others tell you; you are more than just your star sign; a rescue boat. *How can you use astrology in a positive way?*

zombie Emotional shutdown; blindly following orders; fear of the unknown; tired; turned off. *How can you bring more enthusiasm into your life?*

zoo   Animal instincts; trapped; disorganized; under criticism; pay attention to your instincts;   living in a zoo.   *How are you being restrained from expressing yourself openly and naturally?*

zucchini   Feeling squashed; abundant growth; male sexual symbol. *Who is the great cook?*

"The dream is a little hidden door
in the innermost and most secret recesses
of the psyche."
C.G. Jung

Biblography

Birkhauser-Oeri, Sibylle. *The Mother Archetypal Image in Fairy Tales*. Toronto: Inner city   Books, 1988

Bly, Robert and Woodman, Marion. *The Maiden King*. New York: Henry Holt and Company, Inc., 1998

Broadribb, Donald. *The Dream Story*. Chicago: Inner City Books, 1987

Campbell, Joseph, Ed. *Portable Jung*. New York: Penguin Books, 1971

Castandeda,Carlos. *The Art of Dreaming*. New York: Harper Perennial, 1994.

Cayce, Edgar. *Edgar Cayce on Dreams*. New York: Warner Books, 1968

_____. *The Edgar Cayce Companion*. Virginia Beach: ARE Press, 1995

Delaney, Gayle. *Living Your Dreams*. San Francisco: Harper and Row. 1979

_____ *Breakthrough Dreaming*. New York: Bantam Books, 1991

_____ *In Your Dreams*. San Fran: Harper San Francisco, 1997

Farraday, Ann. *Dream Power*. Berkley: Berkley Books, 1972

_____ *Creative Dreaming*. New York: Ballantine Books, 1974

Fay, Marie. *The Dream Guide*. Los Angeles: Center for the Healing Arts, 1978

Fontana, David. *The Secret Language of Dreams*. New York: Chronicle Books, 1994

Garfield, Patricia. *Creative Dreaming.*New York: Ballantine Books, 1974

_____ *Pathway to Ecstasy*. New York: Prentice Hall, 1989

Gendlin, Eugene T. *Let Your Body Interpret Your Dreams*. Wilmette: Chiron Publcations, 1986

Hicks, Esther & Jerry. *Ask and It Is Given.* Ca., Hay House Inc., 3004
     www.abraham-hicks.com
Hillman, James. *The Soul's Code.* New York: Random House, 1986
Jung, C.G. *Man and His Symbols.* New York: Dell Publishing, 1964
_____ *The Undiscovered Self.* New York: The New American
     Library, 1957
_____ *Dreams.* Princeton: Princeton University Press, 1974
Kaufman, Barry Neil. *Happiness is a Choice.* New York: Fawcett
     Columbine, 1994
Krippner, Stanley, Ed. *Dreamtime and Dreamwork,* Los Angeles:
     J.P.Tarcher, 1990
LaBerge, Stephen. *Lucid Dreaming.* New York: Ballentine Books,
     1985
Linn, Denise. *The Hidden Power of Dreams.* New York: Ballantine
     Books, 1988
MacKenzie, Norman. *Dreams and Dreaming.* London: Bloomsbury
     Books, 1965
Mahoney, Maria F. *The Meaning in Dreams and Dreaming/The
     Jungian Viewpoint.* Secaucus, New Jersey: The Citadel Press,
     1966
Mellick, Jill. *The Natural Artistry of Dreams.* N.Y., Conari Press,
     1996
Moss, Robert. *Conscious Dreaming. N.Y.* Crown Trade Paperbacks,
     1996
Pascal, Eugene. *Jung to Live By.* New York: Warner Books, 1992
Roberts, Jane. *Seth, Dream and Projection of Consciousness.*
     Walpole, NH: Stillpoint Publishing, 1986
_____*Dreams, "Evolution," and Value Fulfillment,* Vol.I and
     Vol. II. New York: Prentice Hall, 1986
Signell, Karen. *Wisdom of the Heart.* New York: Bantam, 1990.
Singer, June. *Seeing Through the Visible world.* Harper San Francisco,
     1990.
Stevens, Anthony. *Private Myths, Dreams and Dreaming.* New York:
     Penguin Books, 1995

Sullivan, Kathleen. *Recurring Dreams: A Journey to Wholeness.* Freedom, CA: The Crossing Press, 1998

Swedenborg, Emanual. *Journal of Dreams.* New York: Swedenborg Foundation, 1986

Taylor, Jeremy. *Where People Fly and Water Runs Uphill.* New York: Warner Books, 1992

Ulman, Montague and Limmer, Claire. *The Variety of Dream Experience.* New York: Continuum, 1988.

Vance, Bruce A. *Dreamscape.* Wheaton, Ill: The Theosophical Publishing House, 1989

Van de Castle, Robert. *Our Dreaming Mind.* New York: Ballantine Books, 1994

Walsch, Neale Donald. *Conversations With God,* Book 2. Charlottesville, VA: Hampton Road Publishing, 1997.

Wehr, Demaris S., *Jung and Feminism Liberating Archetypes.* New York: Beacon press, 1987

Wolf, Fred Alan. *The Dreaming Universe.* New York: Simon & Schuster, 1994

Woodman, Marion. *Addiction to Perfection.* Toronto: Inner City Books, 1982

Dream Quest Cards

are 70 theme cards, each containing 5 to 7 questions designed to guide, challenge, and gently nudge you toward an in-depth meaning of your dreams. As you answers the questions, you are led to explore and discover what your personal dream symbols mean and how your dream relates to waking life.

Included is a comprehensive, easy-to-follow booklet: *Guide to the Cards* with step-by-step instructions, examples, an FAQ section, and a list of recommended reading for further study. This mini dream book covers many topics, such as: How To Remember Your Dreams, Recurring Dreams, Lucid Dreams, Nightmares, etc.

How to use the DreamQuest Cards

While thinking of your dream, spread all the cards face down, and draw one. If you are in a Dream Group, or with a friend, you can give them the card and they will ask you the questions.

When you have finished answering the questions on the first card, focus on any unanswered questions and draw your second one. After answering those questions draw your last card and do the same.

Now put the three cards in front of you and looking at the title of each card, make up a sentence using each word. For example if you drew **Object**, **Recurring Image**, and **Success**, you might write: "When I pay attention to certain **objects** that keep **recurring** in my life, I will have more **success**." Others may also offer suggestions.

Describe the object
in your dream
that is most
unusual, special or
significant.

How is this object
being used
in the dream?

How do you feel
in the dream
about this object?

If the dream object could
speak, what would it say?

Where in your waking life
do you have
feelings similar
to the ones you had
about the dream object?

What might this
dream object
represent
in your waking life?

OBJECT

Dream Quest

Describe any part
of your dream that you
might have dreamt before.

How are these
past dream segments
similar to and different from
this one?

How are the endings
to earlier dreams and this
recent dream different?

Where in your waking life
do you experience feelings
similar to those you felt
in this recent dream?

Why do you think
you had this dream segment
again
at this time in your life?

Imagine a fantasy ending
that you would like to see
happen in future
similar dream segments.

RECURRING IMAGE

Dream Quest

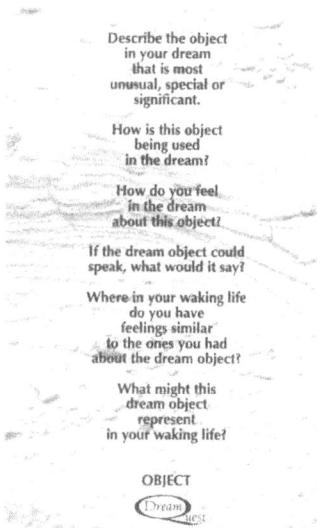

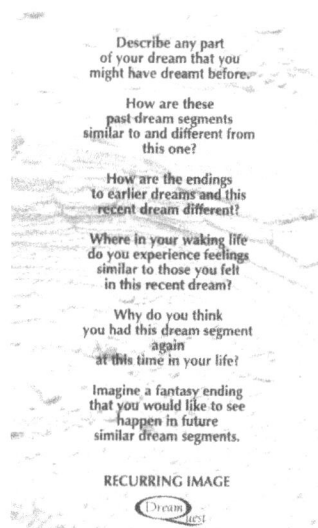

"Dream Quest Cards are an innovative tool for dream exploration, useful for personal insights but especially powerful in group dreamwork. Synchronicity is surprisingly experienced through use of the cards, lending a mystical quality to this non-projective, yet highly effective, method of dreamwork."
Rita Dwyer,
Past President of The Association for the Study of Dreams

"Amazingly powerful, DreamQuest Cards provide a means to access the hidden corridors of the unconscious in a simple, yet effective way." Richard Wilkerson, News Director, Electric Dreams

For more information about how to order your set of *Dream Quest Cards* consisting of 70 large (4 x 6) shrink-wrapped cards with 21 page instruction booklet go to **www.SpiralPress.ca**

Dream Quest Journal

To complement your *Dream Quest Dictionary* and *Dream Quest Cards,* there is the *Dream Quest Journal* for your personal use. Dream journaling is a voyage of self discovery as you open the avenues of communication between your waking and dreaming life.

It has been said that the best dream book is the one you write yourself and that is the purpose of the *Dream Quest Journal.*

You create your own Table of Contents to keep track of your themes, common symbols, and other relevant information. One side of the page is lined for journaling and the other side is blank (except for a short inspiring dream quote) for sketching, colouring, adding photos or pictures of your own to further enhance your dream experience. There are also tips for recording, remembering, and working with your dreams.

The *Dream Quest Cards, Dream Quest Dictionary*, and *Dream Quest Journal* is your trio of dream tools to help you discover the joy of dream interpretation.

Have fun with all of this.

For more information about any *Dream Quest* product go to

www.SpiralPress.ca

It's you who gathers scattered dreams
and shapes their glimmering goal
with spangled self-lit wisdom
into diamonds of the soul.

Nov. 24, 1987
Ruth Cunningham

About the Author

Gloria W. Nye received her BA in Psychology from York University, Toronto; a Practitioner's Certificate in Neuro Linguistic Programming, and the Advanced Certificate in Emotional Freedom Technique.

For more than forty years, she has been studying dreams and exploring what makes us tick.   As a facilitator of groups and individuals, she has found many answers, but still enjoys the never ending questions that life poses.

Gloria lives on a Retreat Centre in Southern Ontario, Canada where she is presently writing short stories and a series of novels inspired from her dreams.

To read what else she is up to go to www.spiralpress.ca

"Keep true to the dreams of thy youth."
Friedrich von Schiller

Notes

Notes

www.ingramcontent.com/pod-product-compliance
Lightning Source LLC
Chambersburg PA
CBHW060247100426
42742CB00011B/1662